APPRENTICESHIPS

Business

Business Administrator

Handbook

LEVEL 3

Published by Pearson Education Limited, 80 Strand, London, WC2R 0RL.

www.pearsonschoolsandfecolleges.co.uk

Text © Pearson Education Limited
Edited by Just Content, Braintree, Essex
Typeset by PDQ Digital Media Solutions Ltd.
Original illustrations © Pearson Education Limited 2019
Picture research by Integra
Cover photo/illustration © KajaNi / Shutterstock.com Roman Samokhin / Shutterstock.com

The rights of Claire Parry, Cathy Richards and Julie Smith to be identified as authors of this work have been asserted by them in accordance with the Copyright, Designs and Patents Act 1988.

First published 2019

21 20
10 9 8 7 6 5 4 3 2

British Library Cataloguing in Publication Data
A catalogue record for this book is available from the British Library

ISBN 978 1 29227 989 3

Printed in Great Britain by Ashford Colour Press Ltd.

Acknowledgements

The author and publisher would like to thank the following individuals and organisations for permission to reproduce photographs / copyright material:

Text credit:
Crown copyright: VAT rates for goods and services,Crown copyright 122.

Photo credits:
(Key: b-bottom; c-centre; l-left; r-right; t-top)
123RF: Mybaitshop 25, Antonioguillem 23br, Rioblanco 55, Gui Yongnian 71, currahee 106, Olivier26 111, Nerthuz 121, Niratpix 137, HONGQI ZHANG 192, Leremy 198, Rawpixel 205, antonioguillem 203, Adamgregor 210, vadymvdrobot 186, langstrup 178; **Getty Images:** Mantonature/E+ 50; **Pearson Education Ltd:** David Sanderson 43, HL Studios 45, Lord and Leverett 77; **Shutterstock:** Niroworld 4, wavebreakmedia 9, arka38 15, Creativa Images 17, Marvent 23tl, BlueSkyImage 23tr, Antonio Guillem 23bl, JohnKwan 30, Jonathan Feinstein 35, Martin Haas 39, Lasse Kristensen 41, Nasirkhan 52, Lisa F. Young 57, Rtimages 58, Blend Images 65, Peter Gudella 68, Lucadp 74, Racorn 83, ZephyrMedia 84, Jacob Lund 91, gualtiero boffi 94, S.Borisov 97, Myndouwe 99, Cristapper 100, Ink Drop 103, goodluz 105, Kiev Victor 109, Bloomua 112, Kpatyhka 127, Andrey Popov 128, Peter Sobolev 125, Aa Amie 133, Photastic 145, MariusdeGraf 139, Twobee 191, StockLite 196, EDHAR 201, Pressmaster 215, Dusit 218, Mast3r 218, Mavo 1, pupunkkop 4, My Life Graphic 5, JohnKwan 1, Anson0618 2, Marcin Balcerzak 7, lassedesignen 175, Paperboat 183, Rawpixel.com 161, marekuliasz 163, boonchoke 164, Pressmaster 167, marekuliasz 151.

Note from the publisher
Pearson has robust editorial processes, including answer and fact checks, to ensure the accuracy of the content in this publication, and every effort is made to ensure this publication is free of errors. We are, however, only human, and occasionally errors do occur. Pearson is not liable for any misunderstandings that arise as a result of errors in this publication, but it is our priority to ensure that the content is accurate. If you spot an error, please do contact us at resourcescorrections@pearson.com so we can make sure it is corrected.

Contents

About this book

This book is designed to support you through your on-programme learning as part of your apprenticeship for the *Business Administrator* and as you prepare for your *end-point assessment (EPA)*. It is structured around the standards for the apprenticeship while all the information comes from the essential knowledge for the mandatory units. While you work through the book you will see it highlights the attitudes, values and behaviours that you will need to demonstrate in your day-to-day work.

Practical help for you in your role

Although this book will help you in your studies, and through your learning journey as an apprentice, it is also designed to help you in a practical way. All the activities and examples are taken from a range of business administrator skills so that you can relate them to your own experiences and learn to grow within your job role – and particularly in taking on the Level 3 role. We hope you will be able to use the book as a professional tool long after you have gained your apprenticeship.

How to use this book

This book has been designed and structured around the Apprenticeship Standard. There are pages that cover the knowledge: 'what you must know and understand' and the skills you will need to put that knowledge in place: 'what you must be able to do'.

In this way you will be able to see how what you *do* relates to what you *know* – and the other way around.

Features of the book

To make your learning easier and to help you prepare for your EPA this is what we have provided:

Introduction to the start of each section to explain what is covered.

Summary text to help you focus on what you need to know.

Key terms – important words are highlighted and defined so you know how to use them in the context of your work. The first time they appear in the book they will be explained. If you can't quite remember the definition, look in the Glossary afterwards. They are all listed there.

Activity – a range of different activities helping you put your knowledge into practice.

Links to Behaviours – so you know how to develop your professional behaviours in each area of the standard. You can use your experience of these to support your work and discussions for your end-point assessment.

Topic consolidation – this will help you to make sense of your work and review your understanding to help you develop in your role.

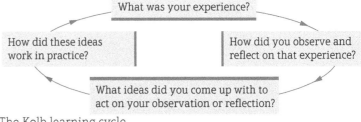

The Kolb learning cycle

Specific help for your end-point assessment (EPA)

Throughout your programme, you will have been gathering evidence from work activities so that you can demonstrate your knowledge, skills and behaviour in your Business Administrator role. All of these will have been reviewed and you will have been given feedback to assist you in the final preparation for the EPA.

Your end-point assessment is the opportunity for you to show what you have learned.

Component 1: Multiple-choice knowledge test

Component 2: Portfolio-based interview

Component 3: Project presentation

The multiple-choice knowledge test is an on-screen test that will assess your underpinning knowledge and your knowledge of the skills required across the Apprenticeship Standard. The test consists of some short scenarios together with multi-choice questions and only one right answer.

The portfolio-based interview assesses your understanding of the portfolio you have developed to validate the competences you have shown. You will have the opportunity to reflect on your performance, demonstrate your knowledge and explain how you have applied appropriate skills and behaviours using your judgement and understanding to explain appropriate examples.

Project presentation is based on a project you have completed. The presentation should summarise the aim, outcome and responsibilities of the knowledge, skills and behaviours you demonstrated throughout the project. It should be produced using using Microsoft Office PowerPoint® or Prezi.

For the full end-point assessment evidence requirements, please refer to the Pearson Level 3 end-point assessment for Business Administrator specification.

Tips to help you during the portfolio-based interview and project presentation

Key tips

- Speak slowly and clearly – do not interrupt or talk over the other person.

- Listen carefully to questions. Do not be afraid to ask for something to be repeated if you do not hear or understand – do not let your attention drift.

- Avoid jargon or acronyms as your listener may not understand.

- Ask yourself questions as you listen in case you need to clarify anything.

- Take notes if this helps you – in case you need to revisit a point.

- **Be confident – you've done a great job so far to get to this stage.**

About the authors

Claire Parry

Claire has 20 years of experience working in education and training across the business sector. As an experienced assessor, she has worked with a range of learners and apprentices across the sector, preparing them for employment and helping them to be successful in assessment.

Claire is also an established author, writing books and educational resources for a range of business-related programmes.

Cathy Richards

Cathy Richards has worked in education for more than 20 years and has managed and delivered training for apprentices over this time. She also has experience of the quality assurance of apprenticeships and is a qualified teacher and assessor.

Cathy has written many textbooks and educational resources over the past 15 years and is currently a senior manager in a college where she employs her own apprentices.

Julie Smith

Starting her career in the travel industry, Julie has since undertaken a number of managerial and leading roles within this industry and in education. As a qualified teacher and assessor, Julie has spent several years teaching at further education colleges across Somerset and has also worked in the training departments of commercial enterprises.

More recently she has been involved in the delivery of apprenticeship programmes for Team Leading and currently leads a team of Pearson External Quality Assurers. In addition, she runs her own business, leading and directing a team of people and delivering a number of educational courses.

1

The organisation

The organisation

Organisations are rarely the same. They each have different key elements that affect how they behave, their plans for the future and the resources that they use. You need to demonstrate that you understand:

- your organisation's purpose and activities, including its aims, values, vision and the resources it will need for the future
- the influence of the political and economic environment on your organisation.

Purpose and activities

The purpose of your organisation is the reason it exists. You need to be clear about why your organisation exists and what it plans for the future, including the resources that it plans to use. The aims of your organisation, including its values and vision, are also important as these guide *how* it plans for the future.

Knowing and understanding the key terms associated with this chapter is very important. You need to be able to talk confidently and clearly about each of these areas in your portfolio interview. This will also mean you are able to understand questions in the knowledge test. The key terms are shown in Table 1 and are explored in a little more depth on the next page.

Key term	Meaning
Purpose and activities	The purpose of an organisation answers the question: what does my organisation do? Why does your organisation exist? Is it to make a profit, provide a service, help a certain sector of society, etc.? The activities are what it does on a day-to-day basis to achieve its purpose.
Aims	The detailed plans for your organisation's future. What does it hope to achieve over the next five years and why?
Values	How your organisation behaves. Your organisation may have a set of values that it publishes or adds to its letters and website. These may be simple words or phrases, such as 'We believe in people', 'Straightforward and open minded' or 'Keep it simple'.
Resources	The elements that are needed to run your organisation, from the computer equipment needed to carry out your administration role (and not just the computer on your desk but the entire IT network) through to the skills of the people who work with you.
Vision	The longer-term plan of where your organisation sees itself in five or more years' time and what it seeks to achieve. Many larger organisations will have a vision statement or mission explaining what it is trying to achieve, for example to be the best in its sector, and how it can achieve this.

Table 1: Key organisational terms

These elements are regularly reviewed within organisations and can change or be updated, so it is important that you keep up to date with these changes.

Purpose and activities

You need to be clear about the day-to-day operations of your organisation including whether or not it exists to:

- generate income and make money

- raise money for a cause, e.g. if it is a social enterprise or charity

- provide a public service, e.g. if it is a hospital or school.

By considering why it exists, you will also become clearer about the way that it carries out its activities. Is it providing a service, selling a product, campaigning on behalf of a group or something else?

Aims

Find out about the general aims and plans of your organisation and how they affect yearly planning. The aims will be tracked by setting objectives and targets that are set over shorter periods of time. They will filter down to every level of your organisation.

Values

Many organisations have a set of core values that they aim to live up to as they operate and carry out their business. It is important you are aware of your organisation's core values and can explain how they translate into day-to-day operations. It will be important for you to know how they influence your role and to be able to talk about the way that you were trained in their use, such as through team briefings or training at work.

Resources

It is critical that you are aware of resources needed for your role, within your team and for the wider organisation. Whether the resource in question is a physical item that is needed in order to conduct business or a skill that someone needs to have, any limits or changes in the availability of resources can have a huge impact on operations.

Vision

Most large organisations have a vision statement available on their website. It is important that you are aware of your organisation's vision and how it affects your role and your day-to-day work. The vision will influence how customers, employees and other **stakeholders** are affected by what the organisation does and can also influence the organisation's reputation.

CORE VALUES

What are your organisation's values?

Behaviours   B

Personal qualities – Shows exemplary qualities that are valued including integrity, reliability, self-motivation, being proactive and a positive attitude. Motivates others where responsibility is shared.

Professionalism – Behaves in a professional way. This includes: personal presentation, respect, respecting and encouraging diversity to cater for wider audiences, punctuality and attitude to colleagues, customers and key stakeholders.

Key term

Stakeholder – Someone who has an interest in the activities of the organisation.

The influence of the political and economic environment

You will learn about the **political and economic environment** in more detail in Chapter 8 when you read about external factors. But you need to understand how these influence your organisation and be able to explain confidently – both verbally and in writing – how your organisation is affected.

Key terms 🔑

Political environment – Government actions that affect the operations of a company or business.

Economic environment – The economy considered as a whole.

Influence of the political environment

Government style and degree of intervention

You need to know how your organisation can be affected by different styles of government, whether it is a government with a focus on private ownership and enterprise or a government with a focus on the state, and a greater move towards socialism.

International relations

Your organisation may trade just in the UK, or it may trade overseas, or it may trade in both the UK and overseas. You need to show how relations between different countries can affect your role, the way you work and your organisation's trade.

How do international relations influence your organisation and role?

Influence of the economic environment

Inflation

Inflation is the increase or decrease in the cost of living (how much things cost to buy in the shops or from service providers). It is measured by tracking a 'basket of goods' to show whether the prices are increasing or decreasing. Changes in inflation affect the way organisations trade, wage demands by employees, the cost of goods or services (both for organisations and people in the street) and how much money customers have to spend (if the cost of essential items such as food is going up, they will have less money left over to spend on other items).

Economic growth or decline

A growing or declining economy will affect your organisation. In a growing economy, organisations produce more, customers buy more and more taxes are paid. In a declining economy, the opposite is true. You need to consider what happens to your organisation in a growing economy and during slowing or decreasing economic growth.

Taxation

Taxation affects both employees and customers (who are taxed on their wages and on goods they buy in the shops) and organisations (whose profits are taxed). Any changes in the level of taxation – whether individuals or organisations are asked to pay more or less tax – can have a significant influence. You need to be able to explain how increases and decreases in the level of taxation affect your organisation and role.

The labour market

The labour market is a broad concept that considers issues such as the number of people in employment, the number of people out of work and looking for jobs, and the training and skills that people have or need in order to do their job. You need to show that you are aware of the impact on your organisation of skills shortages, increases or decreases in staff numbers and possible changes in ways of working as technology changes. For example, developments such as artificial intelligence will have an effect on employee numbers.

Increasing or decreasing costs

An increase or decrease in costs (how much money it costs to buy a product or service) affects organisations and the way they trade. A change in the cost of buying resources will affect how much your organisation must charge for its product and therefore probably also the quantity of products or services that it sells. You need to consider how your organisation is affected by increasing or decreasing costs.

Summary

In this section you have learned about your organisation's purpose. It has covered:
- understanding its activities, aims, values, resources and vision
- understanding how your organisation is affected by the political and economic environments.

Activities

▶ Activity 1: Purpose and activities

Produce a booklet detailing why your organisation exists, including a brief introduction outlining its history.

Add information about your contribution and why your role is important.

Now consider the activities that take place more widely in your organisation.

If your organisation has a published guide, a detailed website or a set of annual accounts that you can access, review these documents and consider your answer in light of what you are reading. Discuss your answers with your line manager.

Now amend your booklet and print a final copy. Add your printed work to your portfolio with a statement detailing the additional information that you now know as a result of producing the booklet and what impact this will have on your work in the future.

▶ Activity 2: Vision, aims and values

Find out the vision, aims and values of your organisation, either by finding a published document that sets them out or doing your own research

Add notes on each, saying how they influence your day-to-day role. Give examples for your points.

Add statements and your own notes to your portfolio to use in your portfolio interview, to help demonstrate your understanding of the importance of these documents for your organisation.

If your organisation does not have any of these documents, write a statement detailing your thoughts on how a vision and set of aims and values could be used to positively influence your organisation. Discuss your answers with your line manager.

Write a statement outlining the purpose of your organisation using examples from its vision and aims or from your sector. Ask your line manager to review your statement and once reviewed add it to your portfolio.

▶ Activity 3: Resources

Carry out research to identify the resources that are most essential to the running of your organisation, such as human resources, raw materials or finance.

Write a report outlining the importance of these resources to your organisation, saying which are the most important and how they affect operations.

In your report, consider ways that the use of the resources affects planning and ways that their use could be made more effective. Discuss your written report with your line manager. Ask them for feedback on both how your report could be improved and how your ideas could be considered for implementation in the workplace.

Add a copy of your report to your portfolio.

▶ Activity 4: Political influences on my organisation

List all the key political influences on your organisation and your role.

Produce a PowerPoint® presentation that explains each of the political influences on your organisation, locally and/or for the whole sector. For each influence say how it affects your organisation's purpose and aims, the way you work and other employees in your organisation.

Using PowerPoint® give a short presentation to your colleagues or line manager and ask them to give you feedback on your ideas.

Put a copy of your presentation (with your notes) into your portfolio with a note of the feedback ready for discussion in your portfolio interview.

Gather evidence of reviewing others' work, showcasing good examples for your portfolio and to use during the portfolio interview.

▶ Activity 5: Economic influences

List all the economic influences on your organisation.

Produce a booklet detailing how each economic influence works in the context of your organisation.

Now compare your organisation with another similar organisation to note how they are similar and different.

Ask your line manager to review your booklet and give you feedback.

Now add a copy of your final booklet to your portfolio and ask your manager to write up a set of final comments to add to your portfolio.

Be prepared to answer questions in your portfolio interview.

▶ Activity 6: Clarifying your thinking

Using all the different elements of research and all the materials you have produced so far, write a quiz on your organisation using facts and figures that you have found out during your research.

Produce a set of 20 questions and an answer sheet.

Ask your colleagues to work through the quiz and see if they can answer your questions.

Take feedback on your questions and revise them as appropriate.

Remember to display professional behaviour when writing, distributing and gaining feedback on your quiz.

Produce a final copy of your quiz and add it to your portfolio with the final set of answers ready for your portfolio interview.

Topic consolidation

▶ Test yourself

1. An organisation's vision helps to guide its:
   - ☐ short-term planning.
   - ☐ long-term planning.
   - ☐ managers day to day.
   - ☐ local community stakeholders.

2. Core values influence the way that organisations behave. A behaviour that would not be considered a core value is:
   - ☐ integrity.
   - ☐ care.
   - ☐ compassion.
   - ☐ greed.

3. The purpose and activities of an organisation mean:
   - ☐ what the organisation sets out to do.
   - ☐ what the organisation does and seeks to do.
   - ☐ what the organisation is considering doing.
   - ☐ what the organisation has done.

4. An increase in government spending can affect an organisation because:
   - ☐ there is more investment in infrastructure such as roads.
   - ☐ there is less tax available.
   - ☐ company share prices will go down.
   - ☐ employees will expect to be paid more.

5. Inflation increasing means:
   - ☐ an increase in sales.
   - ☐ an increase in the price of goods.
   - ☐ a reduction in the price of goods.
   - ☐ a decrease in sales.

6. The labour market measures:
   - ☐ the price of goods.
   - ☐ skills shortages.
   - ☐ the intelligence levels of people.
   - ☐ the number of people considering a career change.

2

The value of your skills

The value of your skills

Your role in your organisation is valuable because it helps everyone else perform to their maximum potential. It is important that you understand how your organisation works including:

- your organisation's structure and how your work contributes to the organisation
- how you fit within your team and the value of your skills.

Your organisation's structure

Your organisation will have a specific structure. The layers within this structure help identify the role of each person and how all the people fit together.

Organisational structures

You need to understand and be able to clearly define the structure that your organisation uses. You should include the number of layers of management in place and where your role is within the structure. Organisational structures are commonly categorised into three types, as shown in Figure 1.

Tall or hierarchical

These structures have many layers from top to bottom. The layers closer to the top are more senior. This type of structure is traditional for large organisations such as those in the public sector or in the banking sector. The advantages of this structure are that it offers good chances for promotion and there are clear lines of authority. However, more layers can be costly to run and they can get in the way of clear communication.

Flat structure

These structures have very few layers. They can result in just a few managers operating at the most senior level with many more managers at lower levels of the organisation.

The advantages of this structure are that communication is often much faster and the most senior managers are more accessible. However, there is less opportunity for decision making and the number of people managed at different layers is likely to be higher.

Matrix structure

This type of structure is less common as it involves teams of employees working together. It is often used for specific projects, with specialists brought in for a specific time. Employees work together based on their specialism and less on their seniority, so this team-based approach can work well where **collaboration** is needed.

> **Key term**
>
> **Collaboration** – Working with someone or a team of other people to produce something.

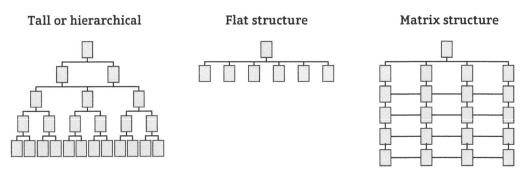

Tall or hierarchical   **Flat structure**   **Matrix structure**

Figure 1: The three types of organisational structures

How your work contributes to the organisation

Understanding where your role fits within the organisation is important so you can see the impact of your role on the wider organisation. It also shows how the work you do affects others and, ultimately, the reason why your role exists!

When you are considering your role and how it contributes to the organisation, you need to consider the factors shown in Table 1.

Level of seniority	The position of your role in the organisation, or which layer of the organisation you work at, will influence how much power you have over day-to-day operations. For example, the personal assistant (PA) to the company director may have a significant influence over operations.
Direct line reports	If you have any, the number of people who you coach, supervise or 'buddy' affects the way your role contributes to the organisation. If you have direct line reports, this means your role has even more importance.
The impact of your work	The impact of your work will help you assess how it contributes to the organisation. A lot of this will depend on the type of work that you do. For example, your job role can determine the type of information that you have access to, such as confidential or privileged information that should not be disclosed to other people. You should also be able to judge what would happen if your work was not completed and how that would affect stakeholders and the organisation as a whole. (See Chapter 3 for more information about stakeholders.)
The value of your work	The work that you do has a value and you need to be able to talk confidently and clearly about how your work supports the goals of the organisation. For example, if you work in the human resources (HR) department, the value of your work is more than just 'administration of recruiting'; it is about ensuring that the right people work for your organisation to help it achieve its purpose, activities and aims (see Chapter 1).
The teams you work with or support	Consider the way that your team works with other teams to provide them with support and to work with them effectively. A team can play an important role in the success of the organisation if it is at the heart of a lot of the organisation's activities. There are common barriers to good teamworking, including poor communication, weak aims, poor teamworking and poor leadership. You should have an opinion about how your team could overcome these barriers and be able to discuss examples to show your thinking.

Table 1: Factors to consider when thinking about the contribution of your role to the organisation

Responsibility – Demonstrates taking responsibility for team performance and quality of projects delivered. Takes a clear interest in seeing that projects are successfully completed and customer requests handled appropriately. Takes initiative to develop own and others' skills and behaviours.

How you fit in your team and the value of your skills

Your organisation almost certainly has teams operating within it, so it is important that you understand how you fit within your team and the value of your skills to the team.

Behaviours **B**

Personal qualities – Shows exemplary qualities that are valued including integrity, reliability, self-motivation, being proactive and a positive attitude. Motivates others where responsibility is shared.

Teams

To understand your role in a team, you will need to consider all the different roles in the team. This should include the job titles, what each role does and the work of the team as a whole. If possible, and only with the permission of your line manager, you should access the job descriptions of all the members of your team to see how each role fits into both the team and the organisation.

Within your team, you should also consider your seniority and the level of delegated authority you have.

- Do you manage others in the team or do you work to support others?

- How much flexibility with your work do you have in the team?

- Who directs your work within the team?

- Who can help you with your work?

Skills

Reviewing job descriptions or team members' role profiles (only with the permission of your line manager) will help you consider the different skills of the team as they are usually accompanied by a person specification. The person specification states the skills, knowledge, expertise and qualifications required to undertake a particular role.

Consider how your skills match your role but also compare your skills with other team members to show the training that you have had compared with them. If you compare your training and skills against other people in your team and then look at the gaps, you will see which skills you have that make you unique.

You will also be able to identify the skills that you may need to develop in order to help you create a training plan and acquire more skills or qualifications. You can then discuss your ideas with your line manager as part of your appraisal or professional development conversation.

Summary

In this section you have learned about organisational structure. It has covered:
- understanding how your work benefits the organisation
- knowing how you fit within your team
- recognising how your skills can help you develop your career.

Activities

▶ Activity 1: Organisational structure

Access a copy of your organisation's structure chart.

Add notes to the structure chart to show where your role sits within the organisation and why it is important there.

Produce a written statement detailing the type of structure that your organisation has and the advantages and disadvantages of that structure.

Ask your line manager to review your statement and, once reviewed, add it to your portfolio.

▶ Activity 2: The value and impact of your role

Look at your job description. Produce a table showing each of the elements of your job description and how they add value to and impact the organisation.

Add another column to the table that details what could happen if you did not undertake your work and how it would affect the organisation.

Discuss your completed table with your line manager and write a witness statement detailing your discussions. Add the table and statement to your portfolio.

▶ Activity 3: Team roles and skills

List all the members of your work team.

Produce a poster showing the specific role of each of the members.

Add further notes to the poster with information about the specific skills that each member of the team has that make them unique or required by the team. Consider whether there are any skills that the team members all have and if there are any that specific people within the team have that makes them different.

Ask your team members to review your poster and give you feedback on what your poster shows. Note down their views.

Write a statement to go with your poster that details what you have learned about your skills and how they compare with others in the team. Give judgements as much as possible in preparation for your portfolio interview and then add both pieces of evidence to your portfolio.

▶ Activity 4: Working with other teams

Think of all the other teams that you work with in your organisation.

Consider how your team and your individual role supports those other teams.

What would happen if the communication between your team and other teams in the organisation was poor?

How could you communicate even more effectively between teams and what are the barriers to good communication in your workplace?

Which skills would you or other team members need to improve communication at work?

Write a reflective summary of your thoughts with three recommendations for ways to improve.

Discuss your ideas with your line manager and add your summary to your portfolio.

Topic consolidation

▶ Test yourself

1. An organisational structure helps to organise:
    - ☐ promotional opportunities.
    - ☐ disciplinary action.
    - ☐ levels of management.
    - ☐ stakeholder arrangements.

2. One advantage of a flat structure compared to a hierarchical structure is:
    - ☐ higher chances of promotion.
    - ☐ more levels of seniority.
    - ☐ easier communication from the top to the bottom.
    - ☐ increasing direct line reports.

3. One advantage of a matrix structure compared to a flat structure is:
    - ☐ levels of seniority on projects are clearer.
    - ☐ communication is faster throughout the organisation.
    - ☐ specialist skills are brought together in teams more effectively.
    - ☐ there is less distance between the top and the first line staff in the organisation.

4. When working in teams, which of the following is not a barrier?
    - ☐ Poor communication.
    - ☐ Personality clashes between team members
    - ☐ Unclear targets
    - ☐ Adequate leadership

5. Understanding your role in the team is important because:
    - ☐ it saves the organisation money.
    - ☐ it leads to promotion.
    - ☐ it identifies the value of the role in the team.
    - ☐ it means that you can cover the work of others.

6. A job description gives details about a role but does not include:
    - ☐ the salary.
    - ☐ the working hours.
    - ☐ the skills required.
    - ☐ the likelihood of promotion.

7. The value of skills in a team is:
    - ☐ less than the value of the individual skills of team members.
    - ☐ greater than the value of the individual skills of team members.
    - ☐ the same across the team.
    - ☐ no different than the skills across the team.

Stakeholders

Stakeholders

Stakeholders are the people who influence or are affected by an organisation or have another interest in its success. The needs of stakeholders are complex as each type of stakeholder has their own personal needs and wants which they believe are the most important. Different types of stakeholder may also be in conflict with each other, so their expectations need to be managed to avoid difficulties that could negatively affect the organisation. To help you perform even better in your role, this chapter will help you understand:

• how to manage stakeholders

• the principles of stakeholder management.

How to manage stakeholders (1)

Stakeholders are individuals or groups that have influence over or an interest in the activities of an organisation. These interests include an interest in day-to-day operations and whether or not the organisation is successful.

The different types of stakeholders

Behaviours

Professionalism – Behaves in a professional way. This includes: personal presentation, respect, respecting and encouraging diversity to cater for wider audiences, punctuality and attitude to colleagues, customers and key stakeholders. Adheres to the organisation's code of conduct for professional use of social media. Acts as a role model, contributing to team cohesion and productivity – representing the positive aspects of team culture and respectfully challenging inappropriate prevailing cultures.

Although all stakeholders have an interest or influence on an organisation, the type, effect and impact of their influence on the way an organisation operates can be very different. Some stakeholders are powerful and have a huge impact on the way an organisation operates. Other stakeholders have little influence and their actions have little impact.

It is important for all organisations, regardless of their type, to understand who their stakeholders are and how these stakeholders can be managed. Broadly speaking, stakeholders can be split into two types.

- **Internal stakeholders** influence and are directly affected by an organisation. They include owners and employees.

- **External stakeholders** influence but are not always affected by an organisation. They include the local community and government.

Managing the expectations of these different types of stakeholder is important, as what one group wants is not necessarily the same as what another wants.

It is important to recognise that both types of stakeholder can be based either inside or outside the UK. In the modern world, international commerce is commonplace. A company's owners may be based abroad or the organisation may have offices in different countries around the world. And external stakeholders might include not just people in the local community but people elsewhere in the world who are affected by the organisation's activities.

Internal stakeholders

There are four types of internal stakeholder that you need to understand, shown in Table 1. Although they are all directly affected by an organisation, each is influenced differently.

All employees are internal stakeholders, as well as representatives of the organisation. When you are communicating face to face, on the telephone, in writing or on digital platforms, you must be professional, confident and appropriate in your communication. The influence and ideas that you express must be representative of the organisation, and any sensitive or confidential information must not be shared outside the organisation.

Owners	Owners commonly start organisations by investing money or funding the organisation in some way. Success for owners often relates to profits and making money. Most privately owned business organisations are owned by people who want to make profits high and keep costs low. **Public sector** organisations, such as hospitals, consider value for money to be a higher priority. The owners of charities and social enterprises will seek success in a different way, by making as much money as possible as a surplus to allow it to be put back into the organisation or given to the cause that they are raising money for.
Managers	Managers operate the organisation on a day-to-day basis. Their needs differ from the owners because they want to have the best salary or overall **remuneration package**, such as a company car or a health benefits package. They want salary increases which may be dependent on the overall performance of the organisation.
Workers/employees	Workers want the organisation to be successful so that they continue in employment. They also want to get paid the best wage or salary that they can and to receive increases in the amount they are paid at least annually. They also want to have the best conditions they can, for example bonus payments or increases in holiday pay.
Shareholders	Shareholders are a form of owner. Shareholders want the organisation to be successful so that they can get a good return on the money they paid for their shares. There can be a small number of them or there can be thousands, depending on the type of organisation and whether they are a public limited company (PLC), which means the company's shares can be freely traded on the stock exchange. (Shareholders can also be external stakeholders – see the next page.)

Table 1: The four types of internal stakeholder

Key terms

Public sector – Relates to organisations that are run by or for the government (either national or local) and are funded through taxes and national contributions.

Remuneration package – The combined benefits paid to an employee in addition to their salary, such as free gym membership.

Which type of stakeholder do you interact with most often?

How to manage stakeholders (2)

External stakeholders

External stakeholders are stakeholders outside the organisation. There are six different types of external stakeholder, shown in Figure 1 and in Table 2, that you need to know about and understand how they affect organisations. Their influence varies considerably.

As with internal stakeholders, external stakeholders each have their own set of wants and needs. Their level of influence depends on their power and level of interest. It also depends on the 'strength of voice' that the stakeholder group has and how organised it is when attempting to influence organisations, for example how well they communicate ideas and suggestions through social media.

Some stakeholder groups can be very influential and can change the way that organisations operate as a result. Other stakeholder groups have less influence as they may be less organised or have less power.

Accurately judging the different needs and wants of stakeholder types is important. Make sure you communicate effectively with each of the different audiences to meet their needs.

As an employee you must be aware that the success of your organisation has a big impact on your own success. Consider how you are communicating in everything you do and make sure that you have the right level of authority when communicating with different groups of stakeholders.

If you are unsure how to answer a question from a stakeholder group, talk to your line manager and, if necessary, pass the query on to someone relevant to avoid giving the wrong information.

Figure 1: Identify your organisation's stakeholders for each of these categories

Customers/ clients	Customers and clients want great service or products that are good value for money at the best possible prices. They want to be able to rely on the organisation and trust the quality of its products or services. The level of influence of a customer depends on the number of competitors or alternative service providers that an organisation has. If there are lots of alternative providers, a customer can have more influence as they can threaten to take their custom elsewhere. However, when an organisation has few competitors or alternative providers, customers may have less influence as they have limited choice and options.
Suppliers	Suppliers want to be paid on time. They also want the organisation they supply to be successful so that they can continue to provide it with services or goods. But suppliers also want to sell their goods or services to the organisation for the most profit they can so that they, too, are successful.
Partner organisations	Partner organisations want to have good relationships with the organisation so that they can work effectively together. Their partnership might be working on projects together or in support of the organisation, through **joint procurement**, applying for funding together, or even sponsorship of projects.
Investors	Investors, who have put money into the organisation, want a good return on their money. There are many different ways that investors can influence an organisation. They control the amount of money they invest and when, and determine how quickly they want to be paid back. Investors seeking profit will usually want to make money as quickly as possible, but if the organisation is a social enterprise then the social cause it supports is usually more important.
Shareholders	Shareholders may be internal or external stakeholders depending on the size of the organisation. Large organisations on the stock exchange have stakeholders who are external as they buy shares in the company. They influence the organisation by attending and voting at annual general meetings (AGMs), where their voices are heard. They can sell their shares, which can influence the price of shares and therefore the value of the company. They also want **dividends** to be returned to them.
The community	The community around an organisation is both influenced by it and influences it. 'Community' can mean a geographical local community, such as the town in which a business is based, or the wider community, as in anyone who is influenced by the activity of the organisation. For example, they might be influenced by the environmental impact of the organisation's operations if there was an industrial accident that resulted in pollution. Community stakeholders are also affected by organisations expanding their facilities and needing planning permission, or if an organisation wants to change the times it operates. Organisations often employ people from the local community – people in this category are both internal and external stakeholders.

Table 2: The six types of external stakeholder

Key terms

Joint procurement – Two organisations, working in partnership, to purchase goods or services at a lower price than they would get if buying alone.

Dividends – A share of the profits that are paid to shareholders each year.

How to identify stakeholders

Every organisation has many different internal and external stakeholders, so making sure that the organisation is aware of them all and what they are seeking is very important. It is important that you can find out information about groups such as stakeholders, if this is required by your line manager. To find out more about your organisation's stakeholders, their influence and where they are based, you can carry out research or interviews.

Research

Carrying out research into the different stakeholder groups that affect organisations can be done using published secondary research data or primary research data.

- **Primary research** is research done directly by you or by other people in your organisation, collected yourselves and on your organisation's behalf.

- **Secondary research** is carried out using research conducted by other organisations. It may be new research paid for by your organisation or it may be research that has already been done and published.

Most organisations use secondary research data, in the form of already-published data, to find out more about their stakeholders. For each of your organisation's stakeholder groups, you can consult already-published information and then draw conclusions and write reports about the influence of those groups.

It is relatively simple to carry out research about internal stakeholders as your organisation has direct access to its employees and can look for patterns to help establish their wants and needs. It is also possible, with permission, to have access to the minutes of staff association meetings or joint management and union meetings.

Research sources are also available for external stakeholders and organisations can find out a lot about their external stakeholders by accessing published material.

To research investors or shareholders, you have already learned how AGMs can be used by these stakeholders to express their views, so you can use minutes of AGMs as the basis of your research into the views of these stakeholders. But it is also possible to use AGMs to hold votes that influence the business, such as on the future direction of the organisation. Research into the type of investors that have invested in your organisation can give more information about the wants and needs of this group.

Identifying stakeholders through research is essential for every organisation if it wants to keep up to date. An organisation selling to another one will want to know that the purchasing organisation is financially viable and that they will be paid. An organisation going into partnership with another will want to know about its history.

Finding this sort of information can be challenging. In your role you should use your skills to carry out research and present your findings in an accurate way. You should review the information to check its accuracy and authenticity before you present it. As a professional you need to confirm that the source of your information is legitimate and avoid any type of 'fake news' or fraudulent information. Figure 2 shows some reliable research sources.

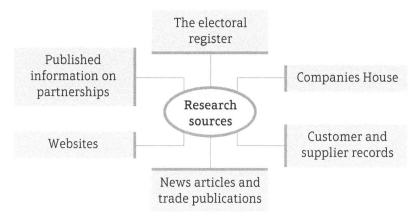

Figure 2: Which research sources would be most relevant for your organisation?

Questionnaires can be used to find out information from customers about their wants and needs. They can provide information to organisations about how to change their goods or services, and about pricing or communication methods. Questionnaires or polls need to be used carefully to ensure that the results are reliable. You may be asked to undertake this task and to monitor responses.

Interviews

Interviews are a useful way to find out more information from different groups. Interviews can be carried out in many different ways including online, in person and on the telephone. Being professional and representing the best image of the organisation when interviewing is crucial, even if the interviewees are challenging or do not answer effectively. Interviews can also provide detail about how the stakeholder groups influence the organisation and their wants and needs.

Interviewing involves effective communication with stakeholders, which we explore over the following pages.

How to communicate effectively with stakeholders

Different stakeholders have different levels of influence and power over organisations. When communicating with different stakeholders, it is important that you are clear about the best method to use and the best time to communicate with them.

There are five critical elements to effective communication that you need to understand and use in your role:

- active listening
- the appropriate communication method to use
- questioning skills
- understanding different types of questions
- knowing how and when communication should take place.

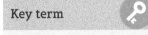

Key term

Passive – Accepting something without reacting.

Active listening

Active listening shows another person that you are listening to them and are going to act, rather than listening in a **passive** way. Active listening requires you to communicate back to the other person that you have understood and requires high-level communication skills. Actively listening involves using the steps shown on the page opposite.

Appropriate communication methods

It is crucial that you choose the right communication method for the message that you are trying to communicate. Table 3 details five different methods of communication.

Method	When this method should be used and examples
Formal	Deliberate communication that is checked by line managers and fits with organisational policy. It may be direct, to the point and 'businesslike', and may include specific terminology or wording that relates to law, as with contracts of employment.
Informal	Much more relaxed than formal communication and may include talking in corridors, sending emails, updating social media or text messaging. The level of informality depends on the situation but you should always be polite.
Verbal/face to face	Communicating verbally/face to face is important if the information being communicated is sensitive or if it is important to confirm that the message has been understood. Sometimes face-to-face communication will be followed up by notes or include handouts to ensure that those people receiving the message fully understood.
Non-verbal	Non-verbal communication means the messages and body language that people give, often without thinking. For example, smiling at a stakeholder may make them feel more relaxed and therefore more open to the information that is being given to them. It is often linked to trust between the person communicating the information and the person receiving it.
Written	Includes all types of communication, from letters through to emails and online communication by messages. It can be handwritten, as with notes from a meeting, or be part of promotional information, for example posters, newsletters or magazines.

Table 3: Five methods of communication

Active listening

Step 1: Give your full attention
Look directly at the person you are speaking with and watch their body language. Avoid looking at anything else that might distract you.

Step 2: Show that you are listening
Give signs to the person that you are speaking to by nodding, smiling or using other gestures that show that you are listening.

Step 3: Provide feedback without judgement
Reflect back to the person what they are saying to you by summarising their comments. Do not add your own judgement – this shows you are listening to their viewpoint.

Step 4: Respond respectfully
Give honest feedback in your response after the person has finished speaking. Make sure the feedback is given in a way you would expect to receive feedback.

Questioning

Questions can be used to get information from stakeholders for lots of different purposes. Questions can be used in person, in writing, over the telephone, online or through social media.

In your role, you need to think about the type of question you should use to obtain the information you require and the most appropriate method to get it. Obtaining information from different stakeholders can help your organisation plan for the future.

You may be asked in your administration role to review questions that are put to the organisation through social media, or to ask questions yourself in order to prompt stakeholder engagement. Forums and social media platforms such as Twitter all enable stakeholder groups to communicate with each other more easily. Customers are able to ask questions and receive responses almost instantaneously.

Questions can be used in many different ways depending on the situation and the **formality** of what is required. There are four key ways that questioning is used at work, shown in Figure 3.

Key term

Formality – In business, means how traditional or conventional the conduct or situation must be.

Opening conversations

Starting or opening conversations at work is essential to your role. You should be able to open conversations with customers, other employees, your line manager and stakeholders. Some people find it more difficult to start conversations than others. If you find it challenging to do, practise it – when stakeholders visit your organisation or attend events, it is important that you can open a conversation effectively.

Questions can be used to open conversations with stakeholders, from practical ones ('How can I help you?' and 'Who are you here to see?') to less formal ones that can help put the stakeholder at ease ('How was your journey?').

Always show stakeholders that you are interested in what they are saying. This conveys your professionalism and gives a good impression of your organisation.

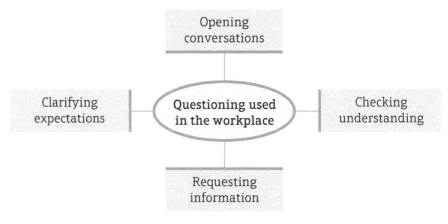

Figure 3: Four ways of using questioning

Checking understanding

Questions can also be used to check understanding in a situation. There are many techniques that can be used to ensure that your understanding of what has been said to you is correct, including:

- repeating back what you have heard to confirm you have understood what has been said to you

- asking a follow-up question

- adding feeling to statements and repeating them back – this is particularly useful if you are communicating with angry stakeholders.

Confirming that you understand the information you are given is crucial to your role. After a verbal conversation, if something is unclear then follow it up with a written response to avoid confusion. In meetings, if you do not understand what is being said, ask for clarification.

Requesting information

Gathering information at work through questions requires data collection to be effective and accurate. Business decisions will be made on that information. In your role as a business administrator, keeping accurate, timely and detailed records is important. Information you have gathered should be reliable and useful for your organisation. You may need to present information in different formats, such as charts or graphs. Keeping the data secure and clearly filed (on paper or electronically) is essential.

Questions can also be used to request information from stakeholders such as local community groups, suppliers or public sector organisations like government agencies. Public sector organisations have to provide information requested because of the Freedom of Information Act 2000. Requests for information can be made under this act, for example asking how much was spent on a particular service. It is really important to think carefully about the question you are asking so that the answer you receive contains the information you need.

Clarifying expectations

Questions can also be used to clarify stakeholders' expectations. For example, you can ask questions to clarify delivery dates for products, costs of a service or levels of customer service. Using questions to clarify expectations can have a pattern.

- Repeat back what you understand about what the stakeholder is expecting.

- Ask further questions.

- Summarise with: 'My understanding of what you are saying is …'.

When you are clarifying expectations, it is important that you admit if you do not understand what is being communicated. Acting on part or misunderstood information is worse than not acting at all, as you may be giving the wrong information!

Types of questions

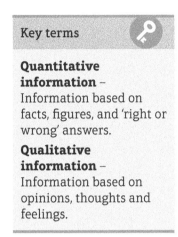

Key terms

Quantitative information – Information based on facts, figures, and 'right or wrong' answers.

Qualitative information – Information based on opinions, thoughts and feelings.

There are two main types of question, shown in Table 4.

Type of question	What this means and when it should be used
Closed	Closed questions are those that have a specific answer that can often be answered in one word, or with 'yes' or 'no'. Examples include: • 'Is your complaint now resolved?' • 'Can you attend the board meeting on Thursday?' Closed questions tend to return factual, **quantitative information** that is collected in one word or a short sentence.
Open	Open questions prompt an open-ended answer, with no single or defined answer. They cannot be answered with a single word. Examples include: • 'How can we improve administration in the workplace?' • 'How do we ensure that data is stored effectively?' Open questions tend to encourage the person answering to give more **qualitative information** that can then be followed up on.

Table 4: Types of questions

How and when communication takes place

You may have noticed at work that problems associated with communication are not necessarily that the information communicated is wrong, but that the timing of that information was too early, too late or did not happen at all. It is crucial that you ensure your stakeholders know how and when they are going to receive information.

Internal stakeholders, such as employees or managers, are likely to need daily information to help them carry out their roles effectively. In your business administration role, you may need to send out daily briefing emails to let the workforce know what is happening. In your organisation you may also have newsletters or team meetings to keep everyone up to date on news and events.

For external stakeholders, such as customers or suppliers, communication may be through social media channels, through printed media such as newspapers, through flyers, catalogues or posters, or by text messages and emails.

Many organisations draw up a communications plan that outlines any upcoming messages that must be got across to their stakeholders and outlines how and when these messages will be told, anticipating possible reactions and queries.

Being clear about communication is critical and ensures everyone is kept informed.

Stakeholder wants and needs

All stakeholder groups have different wants and needs which depend on what they expect the outcome to be from the interactions they have with the organisation.

The type of needs and wants of a stakeholder will depend on whether they are an internal or external stakeholder. But individuals within different stakeholder groups will also have their own personal wants and needs, which may be slightly different than those of the group they belong to.

Examples of the wants and needs of different types of stakeholder are shown in Table 5 and Table 6.

Owners	Managers	Workers/employees	Shareholders
Want the organisation to: • expand • make a profit or surplus • be successful.	Want to: • be well rewarded • feel secure in their role.	Want to: • receive the best possible pay and working conditions or profit share • feel their job is safe.	Want to: • receive the best return on their shares through high profits or from the share price increasing • receive regular communication.

Table 5: Wants and needs of internal stakeholders

Customers/clients	Want the best service for the best price – but not necessarily the cheapest. They also want reliability.
Suppliers	Want to supply the best goods and/or services. They need to be paid promptly so that they can pay their own suppliers and other bills.
Partner organisations	Want to work effectively together and have good communication. They need success.
Investors	Want a good return on their investment through positive outcomes or profits. They need regular updates on the organisation's performance.
Shareholders	Want the price of their shares to go up, or for the profits to remain high and costs low. They need regular information about the organisation's performance.
The community	Want to benefit from the organisation through access to better services or goods, employment or investment in local facilities. Communities need stability, for example in employment.

Table 6: Wants and needs of external stakeholders

Stakeholder power and influence

As well as having different wants and needs, individual stakeholders have different levels of power and influence. It is important that you understand who has the most influence, why and how to respond to them appropriately.

At work it is important for you to consider who has power and influence over your organisation and therefore who is likely to be able to positively influence the company. Being sure about how you communicate with the highest influencers of your organisation is critical for its success.

Stakeholder power and influence is affected in three key ways, shown in Figure 4.

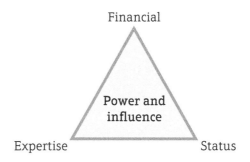

Figure 4: Stakeholder power and influence

Financial

Stakeholders have different levels of financial power and influence over the way that the organisation is run. For example, employees have the least financial power and influence as they rely on the organisation to pay them their wages. They also receive money from the organisation rather than putting money into it.

Investors and shareholders have high levels of financial power as they have often put large amounts of money into the organisation, which can help them influence its future direction.

Status

Status also affects the influence and power that stakeholders can have over the organisation. Stakeholders such as the owners or shareholders of an organisation usually have higher status than employees. Even within a single stakeholder group there may be people with higher status than others. For example, customers who purchase more regularly from the organisation might be given a higher status, such as being invited to events or receiving discounts.

Status gives different stakeholders the ability to influence all aspects of a service, particularly if their views are important to the organisation.

Expertise

Stakeholder expertise also has a strong influence over the organisation. Stakeholders are often experts in particular areas and challenge the organisation to do its best.

For example, suppliers have power and influence over an organisation as they provide advice and guidance on the best way to operate.

Good advice received from expert stakeholders can have a very positive impact on your organisation. Poor advice may not necessarily translate into problems for your organisation, but it would not represent value for money.

Dealing with issues promptly

You will already be aware of the need to deal promptly with any issues that arise in your daily administrative tasks at work. You should apply this same professionalism to communication with stakeholders.

There are four key benefits of responding promptly to stakeholders' issues (shown in Table 7). You must appreciate the big impact of your communication with stakeholders and the benefits of effective communication in this area.

Benefit	Why
Builds trust	Responding promptly and sorting out any problems or issues leads to all stakeholders trusting the organisation.
Builds and strengthens relationships	Relationships can support or slow down the way that organisations work. Responding promptly to any concerns, however minor, helps build stronger relationships. For example, organisations may use staff associations or unions to help build the relationship between two of the stakeholder groups – managers and employees. By building trust between these groups, employees are more likely to feel motivated to do a good job.
Prevents loss of time and resources	Making sure that any errors in communication are resolved promptly can help to save time as tasks do not need to be repeated, errors can be avoided and teams can work more efficiently. For example, if there is a problem with a customer's order, then it is important this is resolved quickly and before a complaint is made. Waiting while the issue grows would end up taking more time and resources than solving the issue quickly.
Builds and strengthens reputation	Dealing with any issues promptly and not avoiding them helps to build and strengthen the reputation of your organisation. This means that stakeholders are more likely to want to work with them.

Table 7: Benefits of dealing with stakeholder issues promptly

At work it is important for you to remain calm at all times, even when you are dealing with issues that mean you meet angry or distressed stakeholders. Always remain polite. Take a deep breath, try to answer questions as clearly as you can and seek help immediately if you cannot solve the issue yourself.

Behaviours

Managing performance – Takes responsibility for their own work, accepts feedback in a positive way, uses initiative and shows resilience. Also takes responsibility for their own development, knows when to ask questions to complete a task and informs their line manager when a task is complete. Performs thorough self-assessments of their work and complies with the organisation's procedures.

Involving stakeholders in decision making

Involving stakeholders in decision making is important for organisations but can also present challenges.

You have already learned the benefits of dealing with issues as soon as possible. Involving stakeholders in decision making can have similar benefits.

Making stakeholders feel part of decision making will help to make them feel valued and as a result they will have higher levels of commitment to the organisation. There are many different reasons why stakeholders should be made to feel valued but the extent to which it is important depends on the type of stakeholder. For example, employees and managers of the organisation represent it on the 'front line' and have a direct impact on how the organisation runs and interacts with other stakeholders, so it is extremely important that they feel valued.

Common ways that are used to involve stakeholders in decision making include:

- meetings where stakeholders are asked to give their views

- surveys to ask stakeholder groups their opinions, measuring changes in opinion over time

- suggestion schemes that can be used by stakeholders to put forward their ideas for improving the organisation

- workshops with stakeholder groups to explore ideas or to discuss any issues affecting the organisation

- campaigns through social media or websites to get stakeholders' views about the organisation's plans

- panels where potential customers can try products or services and give their views.

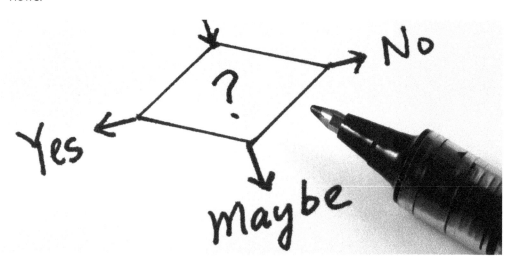

How are stakeholders consulted in your organisation?

Involving stakeholders in decision making means not only that they will feel more valued and committed, but also that they are likely to be more loyal to the organisation. This could lead to their support or 'buy in' to any changes or solutions that are introduced.

Buying in to solutions and being loyal applies to both internal and external stakeholders. External stakeholder groups, such as the local community, can be supportive of decision making or against it, depending on their views. Organisations have to manage those views to ensure that as many stakeholders as possible buy in to the solution.

Buying in is particularly important for future investment. If shareholders are not involved enough in decision making, they may decide to invest in other companies and sell their shares. If the owners of the organisation are unhappy with decision making locally, they may move resources to another geographical area, even to another country.

At work, you will be involved in documenting the outcomes of decision making, such as in the minutes of meetings or by sending emails/letters. You must keep decision-making outcomes confidential until they are officially announced.

Summary

In this section you have learned how to understand and manage stakeholders. It has covered:

- the different types of stakeholders
- how to identify stakeholders
- how to communicate effectively with stakeholders
- stakeholders' needs and wants
- the different levels of stakeholder power and influence
- the importance of dealing with issues promptly
- the importance of involving stakeholders in decision making.

The principles of stakeholder management (1)

You now have a good understanding of stakeholder groups, but you also need to understand how to manage them. A good way of doing this is by following the seven Clarkson principles of stakeholder management, which are outlined in this section and the next.

Acknowledge and monitor the concerns of all stakeholders

It is crucial that you support your manager to ensure stakeholders feel listened to and valued. A key way of doing this is to acknowledge and monitor their concerns.

As well as responding to stakeholders' concerns and communicating with them for decision making, you should actively monitor for any concerns among stakeholder groups. An example of this is monitoring customer complaints. By recognising a problem – even without an immediate resolution – you are showing that their concerns are heard.

For some stakeholder groups, active monitoring may be linked to health and safety. You may be required to produce reports or minutes that relate to these concerns from employees or management. Active monitoring can be done by looking for patterns and making others aware of potential concerns, accidents or incidents before they occur.

'Near miss reporting' is one way to actively monitor any health and safety concerns. This means employees can report (often anonymously) their fears concerning accidents that have nearly happened. (You can read more about health and safety in Chapter 4.)

Listen to and openly communicate with stakeholders about concerns and contributions

You have already learned about the importance of communication, and that decision making is better if more stakeholder groups are involved and the decisions communicated. However, you should always try to be as clear and open in your communication as possible, listening to and communicating with stakeholders about their concerns and contributions.

If you work in the public sector you may need to respond to Freedom of Information requests (see Chapter 4) but even if not, being **transparent** about how decisions have been made is good practice. Sometimes a decision that is positive for one stakeholder group may negatively affect another; for example, not paying a bonus to staff may benefit shareholders as costs are kept low and profits higher. Your role in administration will involve supporting being open about why decisions have been made.

Adopt sensitive processes to address stakeholder concerns

It is important to manage the concerns of different stakeholders using sensitive processes and behaviours, particularly when different groups have different needs and wants. Work with your team or line manager to address stakeholder concerns sensitively, but also to encourage the different stakeholder groups to work with the organisation and each other effectively.

Figure 5: Sensitive processes and behaviour encourage cooperation, negotiation and resolution

Adopting sensitive processes and behaviour will help ensure that, when difficult challenges arise, the most appropriate and sensitive method of communication is used. This will help encourage cooperation, negotiation and a resolution of the issue (see Figure 5). Many organisations provide 'best practice' guidance support that helps them work with their employees to ensure their processes and behaviour are the very best.

When there are sensitive negotiations taking place, stakeholders may be upset or angry. It is important that you display professionalism at all times. Be polite, challenge any rudeness appropriately and call for help if you feel the situation is getting too tense.

You may find yourself in sensitive situations. For example, you may have to take notes during a meeting with an employee, take minutes in a disciplinary hearing or respond to correspondence from an unhappy supplier within a specified time frame. You may be required to take telephone calls or work with stakeholders who are angry. In all these cases, your positive behaviour can help defuse an otherwise tense situation.

Encouraging different stakeholder groups to cooperate and avoid any concerns, such as industrial action, means ensuring that the behaviour of stakeholder groups towards each other is also sensitive. Consider the three scenarios below.

- Employees are informed by text message that there will be redundancies made in the next 12 months.

- Information is leaked on social media that there is a problem with a product that may affect sales. This information is shared widely before staff are officially made aware.

- Discussions regarding the annual pay rise indicate that it will be 2 per cent but the organisation can only afford 1.5 per cent. Unions are asking their members for their views and will have a meeting with management.

For each of the above scenarios, ask yourself these questions:

1. Is the process and behaviour sensitive to the stakeholder group?

2. Does the process and behaviour encourage cooperation and negotiation?

3. Is this process and behaviour likely to lead to the situation being resolved effectively?

The principles of stakeholder management (2)

At work you may find yourself in challenging situations where different stakeholders are distressed or unhappy. You will need to demonstrate resilience and positively influence the situation, for example by clarifying points for the minutes or notes.

Recognise the interdependence of efforts and rewards among stakeholders

Motivation is commonly thought of as a way to increase employee productivity: a motivated employee will work harder. However, motivation can relate to other stakeholders too, such as owners or investors. Owners can be motivated by higher profits, a bigger return on their investment or increased share prices; if the organisation is a social enterprise, they could be motivated by the investment of additional finance or increased interest in the organisation.

If all stakeholders are feeling positive, motivated and that their efforts are recognised, they are more likely to help the organisation do well and to grow. When all of the stakeholders are 'pulling in the same direction', the positive outcomes benefit them all because:

- suppliers get more orders
- employees get an increase in pay
- managers get a bonus
- the local community gets more investment
- shareholders get a share of more profit
- customers get great service or goods.

Work to ensure that risks and harms arising from activities are minimised, avoided or compensated

Risk and **harm** relate to any type of negative impact on stakeholders. However, an organisation can reduce the level of risk by **mitigating** the risk and avoiding harm. This is easier to achieve when you are working cooperatively with all of the organisation's stakeholders, whether individuals or groups: working together to reduce the impact of activities means that the organisation is as efficient as possible.

By managing stakeholders in your organisation carefully and considering risks, the chances of any group being harmed are reduced. For example, a food company that discovers a processing problem will issue a warning or recall notice asking customers to return or destroy any contaminated items. Doing this reduces the risk of someone eating the food (mitigation) and tries to avoid harm.

If a stakeholder (customer or supplier) does suffer harm, they will need to be provided with compensation.

Key terms

Risk – The potential to expose someone or something to danger or loss.

Harm – The damage done to someone or something that has suffered injury, maltreatment or loss.

Mitigation – Acting to reduce the chances of something bad happening.

Issues discovered with food products are mitigated by a prompt product recall that minimises risks and harms.

Avoid activities that might put human rights at risk

Above all else, every organisation should avoid putting human rights at risk. These rights include:

- the right to life
- the right to respect for private and family life
- the right to personal liberty
- the right not to be tortured
- the right to a fair trial
- the right to freedom of religion and belief

- other rights, such as the right to not be discriminated against, access to education, freedom of expression and protection of property.

The UK is governed by the Human Rights Act 1998. All stakeholder groups are entitled to be protected from activities that might put their human rights at risk. This means that stakeholder management must make sure that the organisation avoids being involved in any activity that might jeopardise these rights.

Acknowledge potential conflicts between stakeholders

Acknowledging potential conflict between different groups is important and a part of good stakeholder management.

Conflicts or potential conflicts need to be identified and addressed as early as possible. This helps to encourage and support resolutions, rather than having continual disagreements or problems. This can be done through good communication, clear report writing, sharing of information about situations, compensation and incentives (where appropriate), or asking other groups or agencies to be involved in the situation to help provide a resolution.

Stakeholder groups may be extremely passionate about their point of view so you will need to influence them as positively as you can.

Key term

Conflict – A serious disagreement between two parties.

Summary

In this section you have learned the principles of stakeholder management. It has covered:
- the seven Clarkson principles of stakeholder management.

Activities

▶ **Activity 1: Understanding stakeholders**

Produce a poster showing the different internal and external stakeholders for your organisation, demonstrating how the different stakeholder groups have different influences on the organisation.

With your line manager, discuss the influence that each of these internal and external stakeholders has on your organisation, leading to a witness statement to prove you understand the difference between the two types and their impact on your organisation.

▶ **Activity 2: Understanding stakeholders and their influence**

Read this scenario about a restaurant chain requiring administrative support.

Zippy's Restaurants are a small chain of cafés serving breakfasts and lunches. They are all based in residential areas, opening each day at 7 a.m. for breakfast and closing at 4 p.m. after the lunch service. The owners of Zippy's, Linda and David, want to extend the opening hours to 9 p.m. each day to increase the amount of money they can make and the number of customers.

You are going to support them with the administration behind this change in working hours and practice. Before you can start arranging the changes you must first identify:

1. the stakeholders who will be affected by this change in working hours

2. the influence of the stakeholders

3. the possible benefits to stakeholders of the changes

4. the possible concerns of stakeholders about the changes.

Explain to Linda and David the potential risks of making this change and how it could affect the organisation going forward.

▶ **Activity 3: Research report**

Produce a short research report detailing the research sources that you can use to collect information about the four different types of internal stakeholder at your organisation.

State the benefits and drawbacks of each of the sources in relation to their availability, confidentiality and access.

Remember to use a formal report structure including a content list, an introduction, findings, conclusions and any recommendations. Use your IT skills to produce the report and email it to your line manager, asking them for comments by email.

▶ Activity 4: Communication methods

At work, you will be communicated with in many different ways. Write a list of the last five different pieces of information that were communicated to you.

Construct a table for your list, dividing the table into columns that cover:

1. the piece of information

2. how it was communicated to you

3. your judgement about that method – whether this was the most appropriate form of communication

4. ways that this communication method could be improved in the future.

Discuss your results with your line manager. Develop some recommendations for how communication could be enhanced in the workplace.

▶ Activity 5: Feeling valued

You are a key stakeholder in your organisation and therefore you are important in decision making. Produce a written summary that covers:

1. how often you are involved in decision making

2. which types of decisions you are consulted about

3. how your involvement makes you feel

4. whether there are any ways that you could be involved even more.

Discuss your findings with your line manager.

▶ Activity 6: Case study

A business selling clothing has just been told that one of their overseas suppliers may be using children to produce their products in unsafe working conditions and for poor pay.

Consider the implications of this for the business and its stakeholders if the information is true.

What actions do you think the organisation could take to mitigate the concerns?

Make notes and discuss your ideas with your assessor.

Topic consolidation

▶ Test yourself

1. Internal stakeholders
   - ☐ I can name the four different types of internal stakeholder.
   - ☐ I can describe how each of the internal stakeholder groups is influenced by the organisation.
   - ☐ I can give examples of the wants and needs of each of the internal stakeholder groups.
   - ☐ I need to review the definition of an internal stakeholder and the different groups.

2. External stakeholders
   - ☐ I can name the four different types of external stakeholder.
   - ☐ I can describe how the external stakeholder groups are influenced by my organisation, including examples of their wants and needs.
   - ☐ I can give examples of how to carry out primary and secondary research into stakeholders.
   - ☐ I need to find out more about external stakeholders and what is meant by primary and secondary research.

3. Communicating with stakeholders
   - ☐ I can name the different types of interview that could be used in research.
   - ☐ I can describe what is meant by active listening and specify different types of question, including the difference between closed and open questions.
   - ☐ I know the difference between formal and informal, and verbal and non-verbal communication methods and can give examples.
   - ☐ I am not clear about how to communicate with stakeholders and need to find out more.

4. Stakeholder power and influence
   - ☐ I am clear about the differences in stakeholders' power and influence.
   - ☐ I can describe what is meant by the status, financial and expert power of stakeholders and how they influence the organisation.
   - ☐ I can describe the four key benefits of working effectively with stakeholders to deal with issues promptly.
   - ☐ I am not clear about stakeholder power and influence and need to carry out more research.

5. Stakeholder involvement in decision making
   - ☐ I have a clear understanding of how to involve stakeholders in decisions I make.
   - ☐ I have reviewed how I am involved in decision making in my organisation and its importance.
   - ☐ I am clear about the benefits of involving stakeholders in decision making.
   - ☐ I need to find out more about stakeholder involvement in decision making at my organisation.

6. Managing performance
   - ☐ I can list the seven Clarkson stakeholder management principles.
   - ☐ I can describe each of the principles with examples.
   - ☐ I know what is meant by the principle 'Acknowledge potential conflicts between stakeholders' and can give examples from my organisation.
   - ☐ I need to review the seven Clarkson stakeholder management principles and apply my understanding to my organisation.

4

Relevant regulation

Relevant regulation

Laws and regulations have a huge effect on the way that business administration is carried out. You need to support the implementation of relevant laws and regulations and help ensure that your organisation and everyone within it is aware of legal responsibilities towards employees and stakeholders. To help you in your role and to expand your knowledge, there are three key areas of law and regulations that you need to be aware of at work, covered in this chapter:

- health and safety
- data protection
- equality.

Health and safety legislation

Health and safety laws and regulations make sure that people at work have their health, safety and welfare looked after. These laws and regulations also protect the health, safety and welfare of everyone else who enters the work environment, such as customers and visitors to the organisation.

The most important piece of health and safety legislation is the Health and Safety at Work Act 1974 (also known as HASAWA 1974). This act is the main piece of legislation relating to occupational health and safety. The act says that employers and employees have a responsibility to look after each other's health, safety and welfare. 'Health' means both physical and mental health. This duty is placed on all stakeholders within the work environment.

Enforcement of this act is carried out by the Health and Safety Executive (HSE) and local authorities (LAs) such as your local council. The HSE plays a key role in trying to prevent accidents, injuries and ill health at work, using different methods to encourage organisations to carry out their activities while paying the highest regard for the welfare of their employees and stakeholders. The HSE provides advice and guidance, makes recommendations and can prosecute organisations if they fail to comply with the law. It works with different stakeholder groups and also reviews workplaces, making regular recommendations and publishing reports to keep improving standards in this area.

At work you have a duty of care towards both yourself and others. This means that if you spot something you are worried about, you have a duty to report it or act to prevent someone else being harmed.

Employers' health and safety responsibilities

Employers have many responsibilities under health and safety. In your role in business administration, you will help your employer to carry out these responsibilities. The following sections look at employers' responsibilities. These may require you to help produce documents, display relevant policies or procedures, or even design posters that will help people in your organisation to look after their own and others' health.

Produce a health and safety policy with procedures

All organisations with five or more employees must produce a written health and safety policy that can be accessed by their employees. Organisations with fewer than five employees must consider a policy but it can be verbally agreed rather than written down. The policy must include three elements:

- a statement outlining the organisation's general policy on health and safety at work

- details of who has responsibility for specific actions in the workplace

- the arrangements that are in place to ensure the organisation meets the aims it has set out in the policy.

The procedures or policies should specifically relate to the workplace, covering topics such as how to manage stress at work and sickness absence. The type of policies and procedures will depend on the nature of the work environment and the level of risk: a health and safety policy in a factory will be different to one in an office.

Display health and safety law poster

Employers must also display health and safety posters. This is so that employees are aware of the laws relating to health and safety and know their own responsibilities and who they should speak to at work if they are worried.

The Health and Safety Information for Employees Regulations 1989 require employers to display either an HSE-approved health and safety law poster or a poster with the same content that they have designed themselves. Alternatively, they may give employees a leaflet of their own design that again contains all the relevant information.

Comply with health and safety inspections

Employers must also comply with external health and safety inspections. Depending on where you work and the type of inspection, these inspections may be carried out by the local fire and rescue service as part of the local authority or by the HSE.

Fire and rescue services carry out inspections to give guidance and advice on how to improve safety in the work environment, including fire safety. Their inspections are carried out by fire safety enforcement officers who review the organisation's paperwork and buildings to confirm that every possible risk to health has been thought about and addressed. They also look at how the organisation is managing its risks through risk assessments – see the next page for more information about risk assessments.

When was the last fire safety inspection in your workplace?

Carry out risk assessments and address risks

The Management of Health and Safety at Work Regulations 1999 require organisations to undertake risk assessments to assess whether or not employees may be at risk of harm.

Risk assessments should be carried out, not just for all activities that could cause harm to employees in the workplace, but also when they are travelling for work (for example by car) and when working from home or in another country. An example of a risk assessment form is shown in Figure 1.

Employers must carry out regular risk assessments to identify hazards, consider risks and judge the possible harm that might be caused if an incident happens.

Key terms

Hazard – Anything that may cause harm.
Risk – The chance of something happening.

- A **hazard** is anything that might cause harm. Examples include a loose electrical wire or a wet floor that people might slip on. A piece of equipment might also present a hazard, especially if you work in a factory environment.

- The **risk** is the chance of an incident happening. It might be very likely to happen (high risk) or not at all likely to happen (low risk). The same hazard might present a different risk depending on its location. For example, a wet floor might be a high risk if it is in a busy reception area with a shiny tiled floor but low risk if it is in an area where few people walk that has a grippy floor surface. Either way, it is still a risk!

- **Harm** is the physical or mental injury suffered by a person in an incident. It could be minor (a bruise if someone slips) or major (losing an arm in an industrial accident).

If a hazard is very likely to cause harm and the risk of it happening is high, then steps must be taken to lower the risk. Often this will involve giving training and using personal protective equipment (PPE).

Risk assessment form

What is the hazard?	Who might be harmed and how?	What are you doing to manage this hazard?	Who will do this?	When will it be done?	Date completed	Signed
Car travel	Employee involved in a collision with another vehicle or person	Employees using company cars must provide details of their driving licences. Driving for Work Policy contains guidance on the max. number of hours of driving and need for regular breaks. Employees encouraged to take advanced driving test if they regularly drive more than 2 days per week. Employees reminded that use of mobile phone in car is prohibited and a criminal offence when driving.	HR department			

Figure 1: Risk assessment forms are used to consider hazards, their risk and the potential for harm. They include measures to reduce the chances of an incident happening.

For some hazards there is specific guidance that must be followed or training to be given as part of a special risk assessment. Following this guidance and delivering the training counts as part of the measures taken to reduce the risk.

Working with substances that are hazardous to health involves a 'COSHH assessment'. This can relate to work using chemicals or work carried out in a dusty environment. COSHH stands for the Control of Substances Hazardous to Health Regulations 2002.

PUWER assessments need to be done where workplace equipment such as a guillotine or sealing equipment could cause employees an injury. PUWER stands for the Provision and Use of Work Equipment Regulations 1998. These regulations require organisations to carry out risk assessments to ensure that all work equipment is safely maintained and that only employees who have been suitably trained are operating it, doing so safely and with appropriate controls to reduce risk in place.

- Portable Appliance Testing (PAT) is a common form of assessment requiring all electrical appliances to be maintained and regularly checked as part of the Electricity at Work Regulations 1989.

Employees must have chairs that support good posture.

- Employers must make sure that anyone using office equipment is aware of the risks to their physical health. These risks are reviewed as part of the Health and Safety (Display Screen Equipment) Regulations 1992. **DSE** risk assessments review office workers' posture (the way they sit), the height of keyboards and the screen position, and can help them avoid injury such as repetitive strain injury (RSI).

Provide health and safety training

Employers must provide training appropriate to help their employees work safely. The Management of Health and Safety Work Regulations 1999 require employers to provide instruction and training to help employees be competent in their roles. Health and safety training must be given to employees at their **induction**, before they start in the work environment, and should be revisited regularly.

Provide first-aid cover

Finally, the Health and Safety (First Aid) Regulations 1981 require organisations to provide adequate first-aid equipment, facilities and people trained to give employees immediate help if they are injured or taken ill at work.

Your health and safety responsibilities (1)

Behaviours   B

Responsibility – Demonstrates taking responsibility for team performance and quality of projects delivered. Takes a clear interest in seeing that projects are successfully completed and customer requests handled appropriately. Takes initiative to develop own and others' skills and behaviours.

Health and safety is not just about employers having a duty of care for you. You also have a legal duty to follow health and safety rules and to ensure that you behave appropriately in the work environment by looking after yourself, other employees and any stakeholders who visit.

Follow health and safety procedures

Your first responsibility for health and safety is to follow and comply with your employer's procedures and policies. The need to do this will be stated in your contract of employment. Failure to follow the procedures could result in disciplinary action, such as gross misconduct and even possible dismissal.

Attend relevant training

You should have attended your initial induction health and safety training, but you must also attend regular updates so that you understand your responsibilities and know your organisation's key health and safety personnel. Your record of attendance will also be listed on your professional development appraisal or review as it is an important part of your training.

Report health and safety hazards

The Health and Safety at Work Act (HASAWA) 1974 requires you to tell your employer if you see something that you think could cause harm to another person – in other words, if you spot a hazard. These hazards could range from seeing a wet floor from spilt coffee, noticing trailing wires that someone could trip over, or concerns about an electrical item that is not working properly. Whatever concerns you have, you must report them to avoid something happening to another person.

Key terms

Near miss reporting – Informing a relevant department that you have nearly had an accident or injury.

Whistleblowing – Providing information to an appropriate body. Whistleblowers are protected as employees by law.

In your workplace you may also have **near miss reporting**. This means that you should report an incident that almost happens but is just avoided. This will help prevent someone from being injured, rather than reacting after an accident has happened. When near misses are reported, actions can be taken to monitor the problem.

If you have concerns about health and safety and you feel that your employer is not taking them seriously, you may report them to the HSE or another designated body for your organisation, such as Ofsted or the Food Standards Agency. This is called **whistleblowing**.

Follow procedures when accidents occur

Sometimes accidents cannot be prevented so it is important that you know who to call in an emergency and what happens next. As an employee it is your responsibility to make sure you know where first-aid boxes are located, who to call if you have health and safety concerns, and where and who to report accidents to.

Report accidents in the accident book

All employers, unless they are very small, must have an accident book that records any incidents that take place at work. You must report any accidents that happen. The information in the book may be used as part of further investigation and to help prevent future accidents.

The accident book must have information about: what happened, when, where, who was involved, any treatment given and by who, and further action taken.

Some accidents at work may need to be reported to the HSE for investigation. Serious accidents need reporting as required by **RIDDOR**. Organisations are required to report and keep records of work-related accidents which cause death or serious injury, cases of industrial diseases and dangerous incidents which have the potential to cause harm.

Take part in fire/evacuation drills

You must take part in fire or evacuation drills as required. These drills are carried out so that in an emergency you and everybody else knows what to do. Drills may be organised with the fire safety enforcement officer so that it can be timed to see how quickly it takes to evacuate the building and for people to go to their assembly points.

How often these drills take place will depend on your organisation and its industry, but it is your responsibility to know what to do in the event of an emergency.

Report of an Accident, Dangerous Occurrence or Near Miss

Date of incident _____ Time of incident _____
Location of incident _____
Details of person involved in incident
Name _____ Date of birth _____ Sex _____
Address _____
_____ Occupation _____
Date off work (if applicable) _____ Date returning to work _____
Nature of injury _____
Management of injury   ☐ First aid only   ☐ Advised to see doctor
                        ☐ Sent to casualty ☐ Admitted to hospital
Account of accident, dangerous occurrence or near miss
(Continued on separate sheet if necessary)

Witnesses to the incident
(Names, addresses and occupations)

Was the injured person wearing PPE? If yes, what PPE? _____
_____
Signature of person completing form _____
Occupation _____ Date _____

Accident books are an important part of health and safety arrangements.

You should review whether you, other employees or visitors to your organisation will need help to evacuate, for example because of a disability. If so, you should complete a thorough Personal Emergency Evacuation Plan (PEEP). A PEEP may be temporary or permanent. It forms a customised escape plan for individuals who cannot get to safety on their own. The PEEP should be kept at reception in case of emergency. Details of any specific requirements that may affect the organisation's evacuation, for example the number of wheelchair users usually in the building, should be sent to the local fire officer for their records.

Key term

RIDDOR – Reporting of Injuries, Diseases and Dangerous Occurrences Regulations 2013.

Follow manufacturers' instructions

If you are operating equipment, you must follow the manufacturer's instructions. It could be that you will be taught the manufacturer's instructions through training, rather than by having to read a manual. If so, you should only use the equipment after receiving appropriate training and under supervision, if necessary.

Manufacturers supply instructions for all equipment, including general office equipment such as printers. Failure to follow the manufacturer's instructions may mean that you cannot clear paper jams or replace ink supplies. Be aware of what you need to know.

Your health and safety responsibilities (2)

How you look after yourself in the workplace is also very important.

Wear protective clothing

For some tasks you may need to wear protective personal equipment (PPE). Wearing protective clothing will help avoid causing harm to yourself through contact with chemicals or other substances.

Store equipment and materials carefully

It is important that you store equipment and materials in a way that will avoid others being injured, either through things falling on them from a high shelf or through spillages. Being hit by falling objects is one of the most common ways of being harmed at work. If you are concerned about storage, you should talk to your line manager about ways to reduce the risk of this happening to you or someone else.

Use correct manual handling

As part of your training and on a regular basis, you should receive manual handling training (in accordance with the **Manual Handling Operations Regulations 1992**). This teaches you to lift and move objects correctly using appropriate techniques.

You should not always carry things by yourself. If they are too heavy or awkward for you to carry safely by yourself, you may need help from others or even have to use equipment to move the objects rather than risk injury.

Manual lifting

Step 1: Picking up the object

Place your feet firmly on the ground. Get a good hold of the object. Do not bend your back while moving.

Step 2: Carrying the object

Keep the object's weight close to your waist/body to ensure that the weight can be managed more easily.

Consequences of breaching health and safety legislation

Breaching health and safety legislation can be very serious. There are four key risks that an organisation faces with any breach. Any serious accident or incident in the workplace must be reported to the HSE as part of RIDDOR, then an investigation takes place. If a breach of the law has taken place this can have serious implications for individual employees, stakeholders and the organisation as a whole, as shown in Table 1.

Key term

Manual Handling Operations Regulations 1992 – Require organisations to avoid moving objects if they can but also to train you how to move them appropriately and without causing harm to yourself or others.

Risk	Implications
Accident, injury or death to workers, customers, suppliers or other stakeholders	Serious accidents or injuries can have life-changing consequences. The most serious is death. If someone dies, it must be reported to the HSE for investigation. The police may also become involved, depending on the nature of the accident or injury. The HSE reported that, during 2017–18, 144 workers died from an injury at work that was reported through RIDDOR. Following a serious incident, investigations need to be carried out which will involve interviewing people, and employees may need time off for treatment. This results in costs to the organisation of lost time, sickness payments and possible compensation payments to the person involved or their family and/or dependants.
Loss of reputation	If a serious incident has taken place in the work environment, this could reflect badly on the organisation and lead to loss of sales or cancellation of contracts with suppliers. Having a good health and safety record avoids this and promotes a positive impression of the organisation.
Closure	After an incident has occurred, organisations may need to shut down operations, either temporarily or permanently, depending on the nature of the incident. This could mean a loss of income and customers, and other stakeholders may not want to work with the organisation.
Prosecution	After the investigation into the cause or causes of the accident, injury or death, members of the organisation may receive a penalty, a fine or even a prison term if it is found that the organisation did not act appropriately.

Table 1: Implications for an organisation of breaching health and safety legislation

- Penalties given by the HSE can include compensation orders for personal injury or costs, community orders, disqualification of directors, ordering action be taken to remove the hazard and publicity orders.

- Fines for health and safety breaches depend on where the prosecution takes place (magistrates' court fines tend to be lower than Crown Courts) but, depending on the offence, can be unlimited.

- Imprisonment for health and safety offences also varies significantly, such as two years in prison combined with a fine.

Summary

In this section you have learned that health and safety legislation is in place to make your workplace a safe environment and to protect against accidents. You have learned:
- the purpose of health and safety legislation
- employer and employee responsibilities under health and safety legislation
- the implications for the organisation of breaching health and safety legislation.

Data protection legislation

Data protection legislation ensures that personal data collected by organisations is processed and stored properly and kept secure. Data protection legislation was improved in 2018 with the introduction of a new Data Protection Act.

Principles of data protection legislation

Personal data is any data that can identify a person: their name, location, date of birth, postcode, etc. This data is called an **identifier**. Companies may also store data about a person's racial or ethnic background, political or religious beliefs, their health or sexual orientation. But personal data also includes CCTV footage, a driving licence or photographs.

The Data Protection Act 2018 introduced a new regulation known commonly as **GDPR** (General Data Protection Regulation). GDPR was brought in throughout Europe to make it easier to move data between countries. The regulation gives people more control over how their personal data is used, such as being told when their personal data is being collected, being able to withdraw consent to have it stored and being able to access it.

Each organisation must have a **data controller** and a data protection officer to look after the way that data flows in and out of the organisation, and **data processors** to work with the data. In the UK the Information Commissioner's Office (ICO) oversees all matters relating to data protection legislation.

Processing personal data

There are specific elements involved in collecting and processing data that your organisation needs to consider when working with personal data from employees, the local community, customers and any other stakeholders. 'Processing' means handling the data either by automation, such as a computer, or as part of a filing system, for example by using paper records.

Personal data must be processed lawfully, fairly and in a transparent manner

Your organisation must ensure that it has a valid reason for collecting the data. It must also make sure that the data is only used in a way that does not mislead or harm people, and be clear, open and honest about how the data is used. All organisations must inform individuals how their personal data is collected and used.

Personal data must be collected for specified, explicit and legitimate purposes

Your organisation must be clear with people about why it wants the data in the first place and have privacy information available. This privacy information is usually published on the organisation's website in the form of a **privacy notice**.

Privacy notices give specific information about how the data will be processed and reassure people that it is only used for legitimate reasons. A privacy notice should be different for each group of stakeholders.

Privacy notices should answer the following questions:

- Who is collecting my data?
- What data are they collecting?
- What is the legal reason why they are processing my data?
- How are they going to use my information?
- Are they going to share it with anyone else?
- How long will they store it for?
- What rights do I have to the data?
- How can I complain if I am not happy about the processing of the data?

Personal data must be adequate, relevant and limited to what is necessary in relation to the purpose for which it is processed

Your organisation must also ensure that data is collected in an appropriate way so as to be useful but also not to be excessive.

- Adequate – data must be collected in enough detail that it can serve the purpose for which it was collected, for example the full address details for a customer.
- Relevant – data must link to the original purpose for which it was collected. For example, age is relevant for personal data about buying alcohol, but gender is not.
- Limited to what is necessary – only information that is needed for a specific purpose should be collected. For example, an employer does not need to know about an employee's prior health conditions if it is not relevant to their role.

Personal data must be accurate and kept up to date

Your organisation must take reasonable steps to ensure that the personal data it holds is not incorrect or misleading. This means that the data may need to be updated, with errors corrected as quickly as possible, or be deleted. Therefore, processes should be in place to check the data is up to date and accurate, to allow individuals to access and check their data, and to make sure any changes that are communicated to your organisation are considered carefully, with the data changed.

Personal data must be kept in a form which permits identification of data subjects for no longer than is necessary

It is important that your organisation does not store personal data for longer than it is needed. Organisations must have a **retention policy** that states how long data will be kept and when it will be deleted or anonymised.

Personal data must be processed in a manner that ensures appropriate security

Making sure that personal data is kept secure is a vital part of data protection. It must be kept confidential and accessible only to people authorised to use it. Your organisation must also have measures to make sure that people outside the organisation cannot access the data. Personal data should be encrypted (converted into a special code) and/or need additional passwords in order to access it.

Regular reviews should be carried out to make sure that the measures in place (including **cyber security**) are still effective, with any improvements made as soon as possible.

Key terms
Retention policy – Details how long information will be kept for and outlines standard retention periods for different types of personal data. The policy should also allow records to be deleted earlier if they are not being used and are no longer required.
Cyber security – The protection of IT systems from theft or damage caused to hardware, software and electronic data.

Employers' data protection responsibilities

There are three key responsibilities that employers have under data protection legislation to make sure that their legal obligations are being met.

Employers' responsibilities are not just towards you and their other employees, but also apply to any personal data they are holding about third parties. Table 2 shows more about their responsibilities towards you and other staff members.

Responsibility	What this means for the organisation
Have a documented, lawful basis to process personal data	Employers need to be clear about why they need personal data and what they are using it for. This means that they need to include a privacy notice that specifically relates to the way data is collected for current and former employees.
	The privacy notice should also refer to how the personal data of applicants is treated, processed and then destroyed when it is no longer needed. Employers must ensure that they have lawful reasons for processing the data based on **consent**, **contract** or **special categories**, such as health issues or trade union membership.
Have data protection policies	Employers must also have data protection policies that relate to the collection of data, how it will be stored, how it is processed, how long it is kept for and how it is disposed of using appropriate organisational controls and measures.
	Employers must also respond to subject access requests within one month if an employee wants to review their data.
Ensure staff are adequately trained in data protection	In order to make sure that a culture of data protection care and control is present in the organisation, sufficient training needs to be given with staff to make sure that they are aware of their responsibilities, know how to process personal data, know when they can share information and know what to do if they are concerned about the use of personal data or require additional advice.

Table 2: Employers' data protection responsibilities towards staff

Keeping personal data secure is critical for every organisation.

Your data protection responsibilities

You have three key responsibilities to your employer and to anyone whose personal data you are holding, shown in Table 3.

Responsibility	What this means for you
Following organisational policies and procedures	You are likely to be collecting, storing, processing, retaining and disposing of personal data. It is your responsibility to make sure you know your organisation's policies and procedures for processing with this personal data. It is your responsibility to let your employer know if you are not sure about anything and to read and keep up to date with any changes. If you do not follow policy and procedures, you put yourself at risk of disciplinary action or even dismissal from your role.
Maintaining security and confidentiality of data	Keeping personal data confidential, whether that is paper-based or electronic, is also very important. You must be familiar with where to store paper-based data at the end of the working day. Many organisations have a 'clear desk' policy where all paperwork must be stored in a locked cabinet, but even if this is not the case you should make sure that all personal data is stored securely. With electronic data, you should make sure that all records are kept secure and confidential. Some organisations may have encrypted portable hard drive equipment, but in others all personal data must be stored on the main system. You need to be familiar with what your organisation requires. You should continually review the personal data that you hold so that you only keep information that is necessary for your role, and destroy any data that is no longer required in an appropriate way.
Reporting data security risks in line with organisational procedures	You must report any data security risks that you are concerned about and report it if something has happened that might lead to a breach of personal data. For example, report it if you have concerns about the security of the system used to hold data or the organisation's website has poor security. Even faulty locks on office doors or filing cabinets present a risk.

Table 3: Your data protection responsibilities

You should keep up to date with all your organisation's procedures relating to storing and processing personal data. This means attending training and following organisational procedures such as encrypting work, adding passwords and ensuring that locks and office doors work effectively.

Behaviours   B

Responsibility – Demonstrates taking responsibility for team performance and quality of projects delivered. Takes a clear interest in seeing that projects are successfully completed and customer requests handled appropriately. Takes initiative to develop own and others' skills and behaviours.

Consequences of breaching data protection legislation

The risk of any loss or breach of data can be kept low by keeping data secure and processing it legally and in line with organisational procedures.

Sometimes **personal data breaches** do occur. They can happen by accident or deliberately, for example due to an unauthorised person hacking into a system, and may have serious consequences for the subject of the personal data. Personal data breaches can include:

- leaving data unlocked on your desk or in an unlocked filing cabinet

- accidentally deleting or destroying data that should have been kept secure

- a hacker accessing the data in your organisation

- sending emails to the wrong person

- losing your portable hard drive or memory stick

- giving another person your IT password, allowing them to access data that they should not

- sending confidential personal data about other people to your personal email address

- having your laptop that contains personal data stolen or lost

- placing printed personal data in with the general waste, rather than in confidential waste, allowing others to read it.

In 2018, Gloucestershire Police were fined £80,000 after an officer sent an email containing the details of 56 potential victims of crime.

Risks

There are three key risks for the organisation of a breach in data protection.

1. Loss of reputation for the organisation

Any data breach is likely to lead people to develop a lack of confidence in the organisation and negatively affect its reputation. Breaches of personal data upset people and can damage them personally and/or financially. High-risk breaches, such as those involving medical records, can have a huge impact on individuals.

2. Closure

During any investigation by the ICO, the business operations of your organisation may be temporarily or permanently closed, depending on the seriousness of the breach and the type of personal data involved. Under GDPR, controllers should notify the ICO within 72 hours of a breach, giving details of what has happened and actions taken to correct the situation.

The type of breach, whether human error or a system issue, will require an investigation to determine why and how it happened and what steps are needed to rectify the situation and prevent it from happening again.

3. Prosecution

The ICO can prosecute people or organisations if they breach GDPR. Successful prosecutions can result in penalties, fines or imprisonment for individuals. For example, the Bible Society in Swindon was fined £100,000 after their computer network was compromised by a cyber attack.

Summary

In this section you have learned that data protection is critical in order to keep personal data secure and to ensure that no damage – personal, physical or financial – happens to another person. You have learned about:
- the principles of data protection legislation
- employer and employee responsibilities under data protection legislation
- the implications of breaching data protection legislation.

Equality legislation

The Equality Act 2010 protects people from discrimination in the workplace and in wider society. It centres on nine **protected characteristics**: age, disability, gender reassignment, race, marriage or civil partnership, pregnancy and maternity, religion or belief, sex and sexual orientation.

Principles of equality legislation

The Equality Act 2010 protects individuals from unfair treatment and promotes a fair and more equal society. The act seeks to avoid unlawful discrimination and provides a basis for action if an organisation does unlawfully discriminate. Discrimination has two forms.

- **Direct discrimination** happens when a person is personally treated poorly because they are from a protected characteristic group.

- **Indirect discrimination** happens when a practice, policy or rule puts a particular group at a disadvantage.

Although the Equality Act seeks to protect individuals from any form of discrimination, there are times when organisations *may* discriminate if it is a fair way of achieving a legitimate aim. This means that there must be a genuine reason for that discrimination. These reasons could be:

- the health, safety and welfare of individuals – for example, if a role needs a certain level of fitness for it to be done safely then age discrimination may be allowed

- profit making (within reason) – for example, if adapting a workplace would be excessively expensive because the work building is historic and protected

- the requirements of the organisation and the efficiency of the service being provided – for example, if the role involves giving advice to women from a particular country then it may be more efficient to favour a woman from that country for that role.

It is also unlawful to make or ask someone to discriminate against you or **harass** or **victimise** you based on one of the protected characteristics. It does not matter whether or not the person does actually go ahead and discriminate against you: the act of asking someone to discriminate against you is unlawful.

The Equality Act protects individuals in many different areas of life and society, including in education, employment, housing, receiving services (such as from the organisation you work for) and membership of clubs.

The Equality and Human Rights Commission is responsible for safeguarding and enforcing the laws relating to protecting people's rights to fairness, dignity and respect. They use their powers to challenge discrimination and promote equality of opportunity.

Key terms

Protected characteristic – One of the characteristics protected by the Equality Act – a person with that characteristic is protected from discrimination.

Harassment – Violating your dignity or creating an offensive environment for you based on your protected characteristic.

Victimisation – When people who are protected from being discriminated against under the act are treated badly because they have made a complaint.

It is also possible to take **positive action**, with under-represented groups being treated more favourably in order to reduce the barriers of access to the workplace. **More favourable treatment** is, for example, lawful when considering disabled people over non-disabled people.

Employer responsibilities under equality legislation

Equality legislation places specific responsibilities on employers in order to support their employees to avoid discrimination. These responsibilities and what they mean for the employer are shown in Table 4.

Responsibility	What this means for the organisation
Ensure equal access to employment	Employers must in all forms of recruitment avoid direct and indirect discrimination, and discrimination arising from a disability, harassment or victimisation. Employers must take 'positive action' before or at the application stage to encourage people from disadvantaged backgrounds or low representation in the workforce to apply for jobs. Schemes such as Mindful Employer and Disability Confident can support employers and employees in the workplace.
Make reasonable adjustments in the workplace	This means that employers need to take positive steps to remove barriers for people with disabilities, for example by providing additional equipment or working with different formats such as Braille.
Not treat others less favourably because of a protected characteristic	Employers have to make sure that employees from different groups are not treated any less favourably because of their protected characteristic. Employers need to be aware how something awarded to one group of people may not be accessible by another group, which may accidentally cause discrimination.
Ensure equal pay for an equal job	Equal pay means that men and women in the same employment, performing equal work, must receive equal reward. Employers need to be confident that their pay systems work effectively so that employees are not discriminated against. In the Equality Act any discrepancy in pay is covered through a sex discrimination claim. The act covers equality of pay and all other contractual terms, including access to sick pay, pensions, travel allowances, benefits in kind, redundancy pay, overtime rates, performance related pay, company cars and hours of work.

Table 4: Employer responsibilities under equality legislation

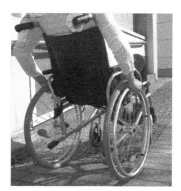

Employers must ensure equal access to employment.

The protected characteristics

There are nine protected characteristics that are included within the Equality Act, referring to the groups that are protected. Figure 2 shows these characteristics, which are explored in more depth in the following sections.

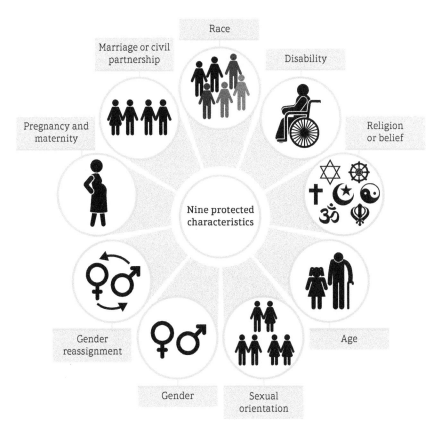

Figure 2: The nine protected characteristics

Age

You must not be discriminated against because you are (or are not) in a particular age group, because someone has a **perception** that you are of a certain age, or because you are connected to someone of a certain age. Discrimination can take place directly, indirectly or as a result of harassment or victimisation.

- Direct discrimination by age would be by an employer refusing to allow you to receive training because they think you are too old.

- Indirect discrimination by age would be the requirement for you to have a minimum number of years' experience in order to gain a promotion, something impossible for you to achieve if you are a younger person.

Age is different from the other protected characteristics because if an employer can show a valid reason for giving preference to a particular age group then it is deemed lawful.

Disability

Disability refers to a physical or mental impairment that has a significant and long-term effect on a person. It may affect their day-to-day activities at work, such as using the telephone or computer or carrying materials. If an employee with a disability is made to feel humiliated, offended or degraded, this would be harassment in the workplace.

The Equality Act requires employers to make reasonable adjustments so that disabled people can have access to work, including changes to working hours, transfers to other locations, use of special equipment or making physical adjustments to the workplace.

- Direct discrimination would occur if an employer chose not to employ a disabled person because they didn't want a disabled person in the workforce.

- Indirect discrimination by disability is an employer arranging training in an inaccessible location which, if you are a disabled employee, would put you at a disadvantage if you cannot attend.

Gender reassignment

The Equality Act protects a person who has proposed, started or completed a process to change his or her sex from one binary gender to the other. It does not matter whether the person has just started the process or has completed the process: they are both protected. A transsexual person (someone who emotionally and psychologically feels that they belong to the opposite sex) has the same protected characteristic.

Marriage is a protected characteristic under the Equality Act 2010.

- Direct discrimination would occur if an employer chose not to interview you for a job role because you were undergoing gender reassignment.

- Indirect discrimination would be if you were a transsexual person and your employer did not promote you because your employer was aware of your link to a group that promoted the rights of and support for transsexuals.

Marriage or civil partnership

People are protected if they are legally married or in a civil partnership, but not if they are engaged to be married or living with someone. If a person is separated from their marriage or civil partner, they are protected until the marriage or civil partnership is dissolved.

- Direct discrimination would occur if you were married and were not offered a secondment abroad as your employer feels the job is better suited to a single person.

- Indirect discrimination would be an employer offering a reward trip for employees to a venue aimed at single people that would not be appropriate for someone who is married or in a civil partnership.

Race

Race is protected under the Equality Act so you cannot be discriminated against because of your skin colour, nationality, citizenship, ethnic or national origins, or ethnic or racial group. As with all protected characteristics, if an employee complains about race discrimination, they should not be victimised as a result.

- Direct discrimination would occur if you did not get an interview for a job because of your race.

- Indirect discrimination would occur if an employer only accepts English qualifications and not another country's equivalent.

Pregnancy and maternity

Employees should not suffer disadvantage because of pregnancy or maternity, nor tolerate unwanted behaviour because of this. This protection applies to a specific period of time called the 'protected period'. Employers also cannot discriminate against someone on the grounds of a pregnancy-related illness. Pregnancy and maternity cannot be used as a reason for an employee to be made redundant.

- Direct discrimination would occur if you were pregnant and your employer did not offer additional hours to you because of this.

- Indirect discrimination would occur if you were pregnant and your employer refused to consider a request for part-time hours, which disadvantaged you.

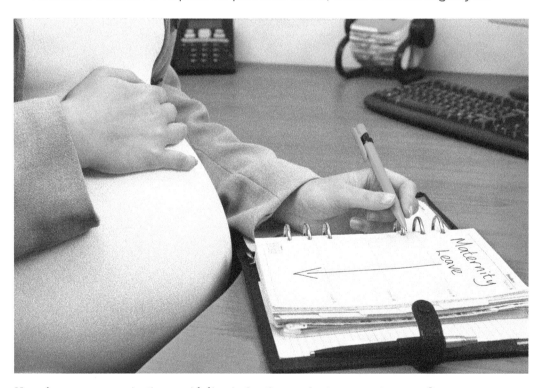

How does your organisation avoid discriminating against pregnant women?

Religion or belief

Employees are protected against discrimination because they have a religious faith or philosophical belief, as well as because they don't. This means that employees are protected from discrimination by someone of another religion, of the same religion or from another practice of the same religion. All protected beliefs are equal, whether religious or philosophical, and no religion is regarded as more important than another.

- Direct discrimination would be if you asked to dress in a particular way for religious reasons and this was unreasonably refused by your employer.

- Indirect discrimination would be where an organisation's employee was unable to access insurance because it is linked to an organisation promoting a particular faith.

Sex

Sex discrimination is not permitted in work and it is unlawful for a woman to discriminate against a man and for a woman to discriminate against a man because of their sex. However, as both sexes are equal, it is also unlawful for a woman to discriminate against a woman and a man to discriminate against a man because of their sex.

Sex discrimination also covers sexual harassment, which is unwanted conduct of a sexual nature or conduct relating to a person's sex causing a distressing, humiliating or offensive environment for them. It also includes being subjected to less favourable treatment as a result of an employee rejecting or being the victim of sexual harassment.

- Direct discrimination would be a job advertisement stating that the role was better suited to a woman, when it is suited to either sex.

- Indirect discrimination would be stating that a job role required someone to be at least six-foot tall, as it is a non-essential job requirement and would discriminate against mostly women, who tend to be shorter than men.

For some roles it may be an occupational requirement and not discrimination to have a particular sex undertaking a role, such as a bra-fitting assistant.

Sexual orientation

You must not be discriminated against because you are heterosexual, gay, lesbian or bisexual, because someone has a perception of your sexual orientation, or because you are connected to someone who has a particular sexual orientation.

- Direct discrimination would occur if a male applicant mentioned his boyfriend at interview and was not given the job on that basis.

- Indirect discrimination would mean that a leisure resort did not permit same-sex couples to stay there.

Behaviours

Professionalism – Behaves in a professional way. This includes: personal presentation, respect, respecting and encouraging diversity to cater for wider audiences, punctuality and attitude to colleagues, customers and key stakeholders. Adheres to the organisation's code of conduct for professional use of social media. Acts as a role model, contributing to team cohesion and productivity – representing the positive aspects of team culture and respectfully challenging inappropriate prevailing cultures.

Your equality legislation responsibilities

Many organisations now have a Dignity at Work Policy which states the commitment of the organisation to ensuring that everyone is treated with dignity and respect. The Equality Act gives you responsibilities to treat others positively and with dignity and respect. These responsibilities are explored in Table 5.

Responsibility	What this means for you
Treat others with dignity	It is important that you treat others how you would expect to be treated yourself. You should adopt best practice when communicating with your employer, your colleagues and any other stakeholders. Treating others with dignity means supporting 'zero tolerance' towards any form of harassment and taking seriously any complaints that are brought to you. You should not use any language or display behaviour that is offensive, abusive, malicious, insulting or intimidating. Treating others with dignity means that you model good behaviour and that you recognise the impact of your behaviour on others. You should have a positive working relationship with your colleagues and treat everyone with respect.
Respect the rights and beliefs of others	As a representative of your employer and as an individual in wider society, you should show respect for the rights and beliefs of others, even when their views are different to your own. Freedom of expression, which comes from the Human Rights Act 1998, means that stakeholders can express their views as long as they do not discriminate, harass or incite violence or hatred against others. If you think that your rights, or those of others, are not being respected, you should use your organisation's policies and procedures, for example the policy or procedure for raising a grievance at work. You should also consider your language and attitudes to others.
Challenge or report incidents of discrimination, harassment or bullying	If you see something at work that is discrimination, harassment or bullying, or something happens to you, then you must report it to a person in authority. This behaviour should not be tolerated. Bullying behaviour can take a number of forms but it may be being: • humiliated in front of colleagues • blamed for problems caused by others • unfairly passed over for promotion or training • subjected to physical or verbal abuse • treated unfairly. Ideally, you should speak to the bully to let them know about how their actions make you feel or ask someone to speak to them on your behalf. You should also make notes of when and where the incident happened in case you need to take your concerns to the human resources department, your manager or an employee representative.

Table 5: Your responsibilities under equality legislation

Consequences of breaching equality legislation

If you breach equality legislation you risk disciplinary action as you are likely to be in breach of your contract of employment. Depending on the seriousness of the breach and your ability to put right the situation, you could lose your job by being dismissed on the grounds of gross misconduct.

Your employer will also face potential action, not just as a result of any breaches that they commit as an organisation but also because of any behaviour by employees.

Breaching the Equality Act 2010 has consequences for employers in four key areas.

1. Loss of reputation to the organisation

By being known as an employer that does not respect its employees and other stakeholders, the organisation risks developing a poor reputation. As a consequence, others may not wish to work for or with that organisation.

2. Loss of current/potential staff

Treating current staff or potential staff without respect may lead to fewer people wanting to work for the organisation. This would make it much more difficult to attract and keep staff. Staff are a key asset of any organisation; if they are not treated well then others may choose not to work for the organisation.

3. Employment tribunal

If equality legislation is breached then an employee can take their employer to an **employment tribunal**. They may get financial compensation or the reinstatement of their role in the workplace if they felt unable to work.

4. Action by the Equality and Human Rights Commission

The Equality and Human Rights Commission is able to conduct investigations into specific organisations, or even into whole industries, where widespread discrimination is suspected. By investigating companies or industries, they can make recommendations about how barriers can be removed.

Key term

Employment tribunal – Can be used if an employee has been unable to solve their equality issues in the workplace. This makes their complaint more formal and compensation may be awarded.

Summary

In this section you have learned about equality legislation that is in force to help to make our society fairer and to remove barriers for groups who are at a disadvantage, helping them to be protected in the workplace and wider society. You learned about:
- the principles of equality legislation
- protected characteristics under the Equality Act
- employer and employee responsibilities under equality legislation.

Activities

▶ **Activity 1: Health and safety policy review**

Find out where your Health and Safety Policy is located at work. When was it last reviewed?

Using information from the HSE (www.hse.gov.uk) and your knowledge from this chapter, review the quality of your organisation's policy and make recommendations for improvement (if applicable) to your line manager.

▶ **Activity 2: Health and safety posters and leaflets**

Investigate health and safety information in your organisation. Do you have posters displayed based on HASAWA 1974 or are new employees given leaflets?

Review the material and make recommendations for improvement to your line manager based on your findings.

▶ **Activity 3: First-aid training**

Review the arrangements for reporting hazards and near miss reporting in your organisation.

Does your organisation operate both types of reporting? What is the impact of this?

Make suggestions about how health and safety reporting and near miss reporting could be improved in your work environment by producing a short summary report. Include the report in your portfolio as part of your evidence.

▶ **Activity 4: Personal data**

Write a list of all the types of personal data that you process at work.

Consider how this data is used and the extent to which individuals are currently able to access it.

▶ **Activity 5: Privacy notices**

Access the websites of three different organisations that you are familiar with and find their privacy notices.

Compare the privacy notices by considering their strengths and areas for improvement, noting the different stakeholder groups that they address.

Review your organisation's privacy notices. Consider how these privacy notices compare with those of the previous organisations.

Consider any ways that the notices for your organisation could be improved and make recommendations to your line manager.

▶ Activity 6: Policy review

Review all your organisation's policies that relate to data protection.

Check that you are familiar with how you should be collecting, storing, processing, retaining and disposing of data in line with your organisation's policies and procedures.

If you are unsure about any aspects, discuss these with your line manager.

▶ Activity 7: The role of the Equality and Human Rights Commission

Access the Equality and Human Rights Commission website (www. equalityhumanrights.com/en) and write a review of their work related to the Equality Act 2010.

▶ Activity 8: The nine protected characteristics

In this chapter you were introduced to all nine protected characteristics.

Write a list of all nine and remind yourself how each characteristic group is protected and why.

▶ Activity 9: Consequences of breaching equality legislation

Research different cases that relate to equality legislation by looking at the cases that have been heard in the nearest employment tribunal to you.

You may carry out this research by looking in local newspapers or by searching for cases listed at your local court online.

▶ Activity 10: Dignity at work

Find out more about policies in your workplace that relate to dignity at work.

Get a copy of the policy and read through the processes and procedures for how concerns in the workplace are raised.

Add a copy of the policy to your portfolio with a review of its contents.

If you don't have a dignity at work policy find a model one online and make recommendations for whether or not such a policy should be adopted in your workplace.

Speak to the person responsible for HR in your workplace who deals with concerns around equality or dignity at work and write a statement for your portfolio.

Topic consolidation

▶ Test yourself

1. Regulations
   - ☐ I am aware of the three key areas of legislation and regulation that have a significant impact on my business administration role.
   - ☐ I can list each of the areas of legislation.
   - ☐ I can summarise each of the areas of legislation, giving examples.
   - ☐ I need to review my understanding of legislation and regulation.

2. Health and safety
   - ☐ I am clear about my employer's responsibilities under health and safety.
   - ☐ I can source my organisation's health and safety policies and procedures.
   - ☐ I am aware of who leads on health and safety inspections in my organisation and what is meant by 'risk assessment' in my organisation.
   - ☐ I need to find out more about my employer's responsibilities for health and safety.

3. My health and safety training
   - ☐ I am clear about the health and safety training I should have received for my role and that it is up to date.
   - ☐ I can describe what is meant by COSHH, PUWER, PAT and PPE.
   - ☐ I know the difference between a risk and a hazard.
   - ☐ I am not clear about my health and safety training or the key acronyms that are used in health and safety procedures and policies.

4. Data protection
   - ☐ I know what is meant by personal data and GDPR.
   - ☐ I can describe how privacy notices are being used by my organisation to help people who are the subject of personal data.
   - ☐ I can describe three data protection responsibilities my employer has towards me.
   - ☐ I am not clear about my or my employer's responsibilities under data protection.

5. Breaching data protection legislation
   - ☐ I have a clear understanding of what is meant by a data protection breach.
   - ☐ I understand the three key risks for my organisation of breaching data protection.
   - ☐ I am clear about the role of the Information Commissioner's Office and how to access information about them.
   - ☐ I need to find out more about the Information Commissioner and what happens if my employer breaches data protection legislation.

6. Equality legislation
   - ☐ I can list the nine protected characteristics.
   - ☐ I can describe each protected characteristic with examples of direct and indirect discrimination.
   - ☐ I know the purpose behind equality legislation and my employer's responsibilities.
   - ☐ I know my responsibilities under equality legislation and who to contact if I am unclear.

5

Policies

Policies

It is important that you understand your organisation's internal policies as well as the key business policies relating to your sector. For your portfolio interview, you must be able to demonstrate that you:

- understand and follow your organisation's internal policies
- promote your organisation's internal policies
- understand key business policies relating to your sector.

Internal policies where you work

Your organisation will have many different policies to ensure that employees know what to do if they have a particular task to complete, as well as how they are expected to conduct themselves day to day. Internal policies relate only to your organisation but cover everything from applications for training to managing absence, filing protocols, and even what to do if there are adverse weather conditions that affect the organisation's ability to function.

Understanding and following internal policies

Internal policies mean any policy that your organisation has developed in order to help employees know their responsibilities and duties within the workplace.

Each policy will include details about how the work should be completed or the expectations of behaviour. Policies also outline what is defined as acceptable behaviour at work but may also give examples of what may be defined as unacceptable and what happens as a result of not complying with a policy.

There are many advantages to having internal policies for an organisation including:

* making sure all managers and employees are consistent in their approach

* providing a framework for undertaking business activities

* protecting the organisation if any legal actions arise

* making sure that employees are treated in a way that complies with the organisation's core values

* saving time – no discussion is required about how to do something as it is already detailed

* providing employees with guidance to make sure that employment law, or other relevant workplace laws, are followed

* helping the organisation to behave professionally, in accordance with clear guidance.

It is not always necessary to have a policy for every type of activity in your organisation – sometimes a procedure or process will be used instead. (See Chapter 7 for more about processes.)

Internal policies at work will vary a lot between different organisations so it is important that you keep up to date with the policies for your organisation. You need to be aware of the internal policies that affect your role directly and affect the organisation.

Although the details of policies may change from organisation to organisation, they usually cover topics that are common to all organisations. Some examples are shown in Table 1.

Policy	How it is used
Appraisal policy	Gives guidance to employees and managers about the **appraisal** process, how often appraisals happen and how the results are used. It will also include information about what happens if an appraisal does not go well or there are concerns about an employee at work.
Training policy	Gives details for employees and managers about the type of training that is offered to employees, payment for that training (if required) and how employees are allocated for training.
Flexible working policy	Covers employees asking to work in a different pattern in order to accommodate their personal circumstances, such as looking after their dependants, e.g. children, elderly or other relatives. It gives guidance about how to ask for a flexible working change and any forms that need to be completed.
Social media policy	Gives clear guidance for the organisation and employees on how social media can and cannot be used. This tries to avoid employees making mistakes that can reflect badly on the organisation and may lead to the employee facing disciplinary action.
Stress management policy	Seeks to reduce the impact of stress (a major influence on working life) by managing the risk, putting actions into place to prevent stress and recommending referrals to other organisations in order to help employees access work as much as possible.
Smoking policy	Organisations often choose to have policies that cover issues related to health such as where on the premises smoking is permitted. They often also highlight any services that are offered to help staff stop smoking.

Table 1: Common types of internal policies

You will need to be aware of the many different internal policies that are in place in your organisation, including those outlined above and others specific to your sector.

Promoting internal policies

Understanding and following policies is very important but promoting them is critical if you are going to have a positive impact on your organisation. Promoting internal policies has several elements including:

- getting involved in updating or designing policies through employee groups or unions
- taking part in training or training others in how to follow a policy effectively
- following policies exactly or making recommendations when an aspect is not clear
- reminding others about policies or signposting them if they are not sure where they are or what to do in a given situation.

Key term

Appraisal – A review of the employee's work designed to give feedback and identify areas for improvement.

Behaviours

Adaptability – Is able to accept and deal with changing priorities related to both their own work and to the organisation.

Key policies relating to your sector

Key term

Sector – A particular part of the economy. The sector may be huge, for example the public sector, or be further broken down, for example the finance and banking sector is part of the larger private sector.

Sector policies can affect the way that your organisation works because they ensure that all organisations in a **sector** behave in the same way. Sector policies must be followed – they are compulsory and often backed up by law.

Understanding and following sector policies

Sector policies are in place to help ensure that organisations operating in that sector behave in a certain way. For example, in the public sector all educational institutions must safeguard children and young people, and in the private sector all landlords must follow policies and regulations about the minimum standards that rented houses must meet for energy efficiency.

Other sector policies may require that all organisations within that sector present certain types of information in a certain way, so that comparisons between organisations can be made more easily, or cover expectations of behaviour. They may say which countries an organisation can trade with or set minimum requirements for employees working within that sector.

Sector policies may be designed to help ensure that environmental standards are maintained.

There are many benefits to having sector-wide policies. These include ensuring that the sector has minimum expectations that every organisation must meet. This may be for training. For example, people working with food must have appropriate supervision and training in food hygiene as part of a health and safety policy that affects the whole sector.

The waste and recycling sector has specific rules and guidance on how waste is disposed. For example, to dispose of certain types of hazardous waste, permits must be applied for. By making sure that all organisations in this sector treat waste to the same high standards, it avoids organisations cutting corners or trying to use the cheapest way to dispose of certain types of waste, ways which may be bad for the environment.

In the public sector, employees are encouraged to join pension schemes where policy rules apply to the public sector as a whole. For example, the Local Government Pension Scheme is a scheme for employees working in education, the probation service and the local councils. All the employees working in this sector are affected by changes to pension policy that affect the whole sector, for example a change in contributions or the retirement age.

Summary

In this section you have learned about your organisation's internal policies and business policies relating to your sector.

Activities

▶ **Activity 1: Review of the appraisal policy**

Your organisation will have an appraisal or review policy. Get a copy of the policy to place in your portfolio.

Write a list of the advantages of having this policy. Now review the policy to consider if there are any ways to improve it, for example if any areas are unclear. Note the date when the policy was last reviewed.

In your review, say how the policy helps you at work and how you follow the policy. Add the original policy and your list and review statement to your portfolio. Discuss your ideas with your line manager.

▶ **Activity 2: Social media policy**

Access the social media policy for your organisation. If your organisation does not have one, source one online or talk to your line manager about drafting a policy that could be considered by your organisation.

Produce a presentation for more senior managers in your organisation on the importance of a social media policy to show why it should be in place and how you can ensure that you are following organisational policy.

Ask your colleagues about their understanding of the social media policy for your organisation and then make recommendations to your line manager on further training or information that may help them to improve their understanding even more.

▶ **Activity 3: Promoting policies at work**

List what you think are the top ten policies that have been approved in your workplace.

In a written statement, review the way that the policies are promoted or communicated to employees and note how often the policies are renewed and any differences.

Make a judgement about the effectiveness of the promotion of the policies and what else your organisation could do to help employees be clearer about them. Discuss your findings with your line manager and practise demonstrating your understanding with a Q&A session. Ask your line manager to write a statement for you on your performance and how you could improve your understanding and promotion of internal policies.

▶ **Activity 4: Sector policies**

Have a discussion with your line manager about the sector policies that you think affect your organisation the most.

Make notes during the discussion and then type them up for inclusion in your portfolio. Ask your line manager to review the notes to check that you have captured all the necessary information or if there are any changes that you should make.

Review your work again in light of your line manager's feedback and add your draft and final pieces to your portfolio of evidence.

Topic consolidation

▶ Test yourself

1. One disadvantage of having a large number of internal policies is:
   ☐ clarity for staff.
   ☐ being more business-like.
   ☐ a framework is provided for the organisation.
   ☐ renewal dates must be monitored.

2. Internal policies provide guidance so that:
   ☐ employees can misbehave effectively.
   ☐ employees can follow employment and other laws.
   ☐ employees can be punished.
   ☐ employees can be motivated.

3. One benefit of having a social media policy is:
   ☐ employees will use social media more.
   ☐ the number of followers on Twitter increases.
   ☐ communication is more effective.
   ☐ employees avoid making mistakes online.

4. Being clear about internal policies is important because:
   ☐ it uses organisation time.
   ☐ it avoids confusion for employees.
   ☐ it slows decision-making processes.
   ☐ it causes conflict amongst employees.

5. Promoting internal policies means:
   ☐ getting an increase in salary.
   ☐ telling other employees what to do.
   ☐ highlighting to others what is included in a policy.
   ☐ annoying other employees.

6. Promoting sector policies in all organisations ensures that all organisations:
   ☐ understand what customers want and need.
   ☐ have a fair chance of competing.
   ☐ have to pay higher expenses.
   ☐ are legally compliant for the minimum expectations.

7. Following organisational policies, for example smoking or stress management at work, is important because:
   ☐ copying others may get you into trouble.
   ☐ it shows employees as good role models and demonstrates professional behaviour.
   ☐ stakeholders may be unclear about the services your organisation offers.
   ☐ not following a policy may lead to an error being made.

6

Business fundamentals

Business fundamentals

Business fundamentals are the essential things that influence the role of a business administrator. In your administration role, you will be actively involved in some of these aspects and provide support for them, or you will be affected by them. You need to demonstrate that you understand:

- financial processes and the impact of following effective financial processes
- managing change and the impact of effective change management
- project life cycles/project management and the impact of effective project management.

Principles of financial processes (1)

Financial processes relevant in administration focus on four key areas: accounting, payroll, managing budgets and any other paperwork that is relevant to finance, such as purchase orders and delivery notes.

Finance affects all organisations, so they need to process paperwork or use online methods to record income and expenditure, and to manage financial processes throughout the financial year.

Accounting

You will be helping to generate records and evidence – both online or on paper – of what happens financially in your organisation. The type of role that you perform will influence how much you are involved in each part of the accounting process but it is important to be aware of all the elements.

Recording transactions

Recording **accounting transactions** means keeping records of all the different receipts that come into the organisation. These might be sales receipts or, if you are working for a charity or similar type of organisation, might be for grants or other types of income.

Costs are everything that is paid out of the organisation. Each purchase must be recorded so that it can be checked through audit (see below).

Monitoring activity

You may be asked to check spending levels within a team or department or by an individual. The spending may have used a company credit card or been from a bank account. You may also be asked to review the amount of money that is available by reviewing or influencing the **cash flow** of your department or the organisation as a whole.

Auditing

Processing and recording the transactions is the first stage that you may be involved in or influenced by. The next stage is checking that they are accurate. This is known as auditing. There are two types of auditing: **internal audit** and **external audit**. Both types check that the financial processes are accurate and that money is being spent correctly.

- Internal audits are not required by all organisations, but many choose to do them to improve or confirm the accuracy of their financial reporting. They are carried out by staff inside the organisation.

- External audits are mandatory (they have to be done) as they reassure agencies (such as HM Revenue & Customs, shareholders and government agencies) that the published accounts are accurate. They are carried out by someone outside the company.

Payroll

This is the financial process that ensures that employees are paid each week or month. Payroll can be carried out through different functions of the business, for example the finance department, the human resources department, by the company accountant or by a third party such as a local authority.

You need to be aware of the administration of payroll as not only could it be part of your role you will need to check your own details.

The tasks involved in the payroll process are shown in Table 1.

Payroll process	Relevance to your role in administration
Creating pay statements	You may be asked to create payslips at the end of the month. Many larger organisations now issue electronic payslips that can be accessed through a password and username, but others still use paper payslips.
Making salary payments and deductions	You may administer salary deductions. This could be for time off without pay or for schemes such as cycle to work or childcare vouchers, or to repay season-ticket travel loans.
Processing employee business expenses	You may have to process expenses for your line manager or other members of the team. You may also have access to a company credit card or be able to raise invoices. Keeping accurate records of business expenses is essential.
Calculating National Insurance (NI) contributions	You may be asked to work out contributions for National Insurance or assist in this process. Employees pay different levels of National Insurance depending on their earnings and the hours that they work.
Calculating pension contributions	You may have to calculate pension contributions that need to be deducted from employees' pay. You may have to seek advice from qualified people, such as pension advisers or accountants, to check your work and ensure that payments are accurate. Courses are available that specialise in the administration of pensions, and other aspects of payroll, as everyone in work is encouraged to be in a pension scheme to plan for their retirement.

Table 1: Payroll process tasks

Principles of financial processes (2)

Managing budgets

Organisations use **budgets** to plan their spending or the sales they expect to make. These forecasts can be used to review whether spending is too high or sales are too low. A **budget holder** may have some freedom to decide how the money given to them in the budget is set. Other people, such as in a sales team, may be set sales targets based on achieving a budget.

There are five key ways that budgets are used.

Identifying priorities

Budgets help focus the budget holder's mind to avoid overspending and help them decide what money needs to be spent that year. Working out priorities for '**zero based budgeting**' or comparing against spending from the previous year can focus the expenditure of your organisation.

Negotiating and agreeing financial resources

Budgets help the budget holders and their administrative team work out what they need in the next financial year or over the coming years. Some organisations will produce an annual budget, others will product draft budgets for three or even five years. This will depend on the size and policies of the organisation and its ability to negotiate with its customers and suppliers.

If you work for a charity or social enterprise, you may need to produce a budget to bid for finance to undertake a project.

Recording income and expenditure

After the budget has been agreed, either for spending to be made or for sales that are expected, it can be used to compare against what actually happens and so see where the income or expenditure is being specified. For example, a sales budget may list a certain number of different types of products to be sold, and an expenditure budget may have different 'cost lines' such as the amount that is allowed to be spent on postage.

Monitoring income and expenditure against planned activity

Each month, income and expenditure against budget is checked to see whether the planned number of sales, income from grants or expenditure have been met. Monitoring on a regular basis helps to identify any problems, such as poor sales, as they arise.

Making corrective actions

Once activity has been monitored against budget it is important that any differences are highlighted. In your role, supporting or holding the budget, you may need to act to correct or address any differences. These actions could be to try and increase sales or to reduce costs in another area.

In your role, how can you improve your management of budgets?

Documentation required for financial processes

It is vital that you understand – and are prepared to support – the different types of document that are used for financial processes, shown in Table 2. Each one has a key purpose in financial monitoring. You need to be familiar with each in order to provide the very best support to your colleagues.

Document	Purpose
Income statement (profit and loss)	The income and expenditure (I&E) statement helps an organisation see how much money is coming in and how much is going out. In organisations that are profit making and aim to make a **surplus** (where profits are more than expenditure), this forms a statement called the profit and loss statement (P&L). You may be asked to help prepare this, usually using accounting software, or to write all or part of the commentary that goes with it.
Balance sheet	The balance sheet lists all the **assets** of an organisation. These assets may be current assets or fixed assets – see the *Key terms* box for an explanation. It also shows who the organisation owes money to, known as **liabilities**.
Purchase orders	Purchase orders are the documents that request to buy something, for example goods or services. Many organisations, especially large ones, require a purchase order to be raised before something is bought.
Delivery notes	When something is delivered to your organisation, you may be involved in checking that the order has arrived on time and that it is correct and not damaged. The delivery note is then signed. In your organisation you may also assist in the administration of delivery notes for goods being sent out to customers.
Invoices	Invoices are the documents that specify the payment to be made to or by the organisation. Most organisations have a specified number of days indicated (within 30 or 60 days) to show when payment is due. They may include **value added tax (VAT)** which also needs to be paid. The amount of this tax will depend on the type of goods or services being purchased. Keeping track of invoices is important to help with the cash flow of the organisation.
Receipts	Receipts are given for any purchase to show that payment has been made. They can be paper, electronic or text-based.
Statements of account	A statement of account is often sent between organisations to summarise recent transactions. They show the total number of sales, invoices paid and any returns (**credit notes**). It is important to review statements of account and to check the balances on a regular basis.

Table 2: The different types of document used for financial processes

Key terms

Surplus – The amount of money that is left over after an organisation has taken its expenses away from its income.

Assets – Resources that hold value to the organisation.

- **Current assets** can be converted to cash quickly (e.g. products in stock for sale).
- **Fixed assets** are land, equipment or buildings that can be valued but would take longer to be turned into cash.

Liabilities – Money that the organisation owes.

- **Short-term/current liabilities** usually need to be paid within one year.
- **Long-term liabilities**, for example a mortgage or loan, are paid over many years.

Value added tax (VAT) – A tax added to the cost of some goods and services.

Credit note – A statement given to the organisation or customer when goods have been returned. The value can be used for future purchases.

The impact of financial processes

Financial processes have a huge impact on your administrative role because their efficient completion helps your organisation operate effectively.

Impact on the administrator role

You can read more about the benefit of following processes in general in Chapter 7. The main benefits are that they can simplify and speed up the work that you do.

But following financial processes can also have additional benefits for you in your administrator role. For example, the security and reassurance of knowing that your payroll is being administered correctly, that your pension contributions are accurate and that your personal information is being kept secure is very important.

If you are not confident about the processes in place, this could negatively affect both your **motivation** and that of others in your organisation.

In your administration role, efficient financial processes can be based on either paper or online systems. Organisations are increasingly using online systems because they ensure that payments can be tracked via email and in real time.

However, moving processes online means that you and your organisation need to ensure that personal data is secure. Consider what you learned about data protection and GDPR in Chapter 4 – there are implications for financial processes, including payroll and holding personal information, that affect both you and your organisation.

Impact on the organisation

Organisations will benefit from financial processes just as much as they do from general processes (see Chapter 7). But financial processes also have distinct advantages for the organisation.

Ability to forecast finances and take appropriate action

Having good, correct and timely financial processes means that organisations can forecast and track their finances accurately. The more efficient your organisation is at forecasting, the more likely it is to be successful at managing its finances and making decisions related to them.

Tracking the finances and comparing against budget ensure your organisation can take appropriate action if performance does not match the forecast. Often the cause of organisations facing financial issues and bankruptcy is not an inability to make a profit but running out of money as a result of poor cash flow.

Allows for accurate planning of resources

Having good financial procedures and processes ensures effective planning of resources. There are three key areas of resource planning that are important to an organisation.

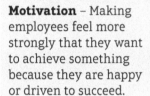

Key term

Motivation – Making employees feel more strongly that they want to achieve something because they are happy or driven to succeed.

Behaviours **B**

Managing performance – Takes responsibility for their own work, accepts feedback in a positive way, uses initiative and shows resilience. Also takes responsibility for their own development, knows when to ask questions to complete a task and informs their line manager when a task is complete. Performs thorough self-assessments of their work and complies with the organisation's procedures.

- **Finance** – having enough **cash** for both short-term and long-term financial planning.

- **Time** – planning how long something will take and the action to be taken if it is taking too long is key to business administration. You and your organisation may need to look for additional resourcing if things are happening more quickly or more slowly than expected.

  If processes are not efficient and information is lost or has to be completed more than once, this is known as an **opportunity cost** to the organisation as other duties cannot be performed. Being able to effectively plan time also helps to produce a quality product or offer a quality service. If there is too little time, work may be rushed and poor quality and this will ultimately affect the reputation of the organisation.

- **Employees** – employees benefit from efficient processes, as we will see in Chapter 7, which means the organisation also benefits. If processes are too long, repetitive or inaccurate, employees are likely to have to redo their work or chase others for information. Repeating work is costly to the organisation in terms of money, and new customers/clients may be lost.

> **Key terms** 🔑
>
> **Cash** – The amount of physical money in the bank.
>
> **Opportunity cost** – The loss of other, more profitable alternatives when you have to do something else instead.

Pick a financial process covered in this chapter and consider how it affects your role.

Helps ensure compliance with relevant legislation and regulations

It is important that your organisation has clear instructions and policies for how long data is kept (retained) and how it is kept secure and confidential. Most organisations have a retention policy for financial data that is six years plus the current year (this is also the standard retention period required of organisations by HM Revenue & Customs).

Having a clear retention, security and confidentiality policy is key to avoiding problems with financial data compliance. It is also important to be aware of the latest guidelines relating to freedom of information and data protection legislation that affect your organisation – see Chapter 4 for more information.

The principles of managing change

Managing change means supporting the organisation to do things differently. This can involve changes to the way administration is carried out, to the roles people have or to the resources that are used.

Managing change

Managing change is important for all types of organisation as careful management can ensure that changes are successful and adopted by everyone involved. Poor change management can have negative effects on the organisation and even lead to financial loss.

Types of change

There are four key ways of describing change in an organisation.

Step change

Step change means having a goal or idea for each step that can be achieved before moving on to the next step. Breaking down change into steps makes it more manageable for an organisation and for the people working in that organisation to understand what is going to happen, when it is happening and how the change is going to affect them.

Step change management's 'steps' include communication so that everyone is aware of what is happening, why it is happening and what needs to be done to avoid that change slowing or not happening at all. Step change also involves 'easy wins' at every step because it is important that the team undergoing the change has success at each step and finds ways to celebrate early.

Step change has been modelled by John Kotter and is shown in Figure 1.

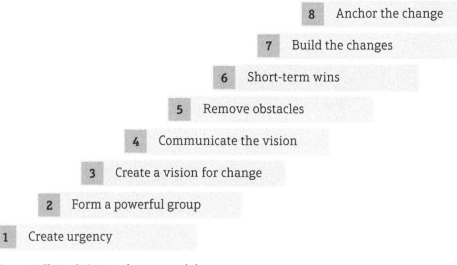

Figure 1: Kotter's 8-step change model

Incremental change

Incremental change means making small adjustments to the way things are done that, when combined with other small adjustments, leads to a bigger change overall. Incremental change, unlike step change, means reviewing processes at the very smallest level. If every process is improved by a small amount, these changes over time will lead to what are called 'marginal gains' that significantly improve overall performance.

Incremental change in your organisation, or even in your specific administration role, can be combined to make significant efficiencies.

Planned change

Planned change has different meanings depending on the organisation and the reasons for change. It usually has a greater timescale and can be thought about thoroughly in advance. There can be many different reasons why planned change might need to happen, for example:

- legislation and regulation relating to an industry is updated and needs to be reacted to

- increasing costs need to be reduced, for example through redundancies

- new ways of working are introduced, such as new machinery or equipment that require training

- competitors have brought out a new product or service that needs to be reacted to

- technological changes are introduced to bring in the latest developments

- customer satisfaction or wants and demand from new areas must be responded to.

It is important to ensure that planned changes are completed as smoothly as possible. Sometimes organisations may choose to relocate their workforce to another town or even country; this is a planned change that needs careful management so that employees are aware of what is happening and can comment.

In larger organisations, particularly those with unions, consultation with union groups and employees may be required if 20 or more redundancies are planned within 90 days. If employers do not consult within this timescale, they risk legal action for unfair dismissal.

Planned change also includes **contingency planning**. This is when organisations map out certain courses of action that they hope they will not have to implement, such as what to do in response to an emergency.

Unplanned change

Unplanned change is when something has happened that you were not expecting. This type of change can be very difficult to manage and tends to be disorganised. Unplanned changes may require crisis management. This type of change may occur because of poor employee and employer partnerships, because of a change in the way a product or service is perceived or offered, or because of changes in financial performance or employee expectations.

When an unplanned change happens there is often employee unrest and employees may try to resist it by taking industrial action.

Requirements for managing change effectively (1)

Change can happen as a part of a plan, in steps, incrementally or as a result of unplanned events. However, whatever the reason why your organisation is going through change, there are elements that can make changes happen more effectively and these can be divided into six requirements.

Effective leadership

Having leaders who provide a positive and professional environment makes positive change more likely to happen. Being professional and positive also makes the change, however difficult, more likely to be successful.

Being clear about what is happening establishes the direction of the change and sets out where the organisation expects to be in the future. This is also linked to the organisation's vision of where it sees itself in two, five or ten years.

By having clear leadership, the organisation can move forward and take steps to implement the change. This makes communication easier and helps employees to understand their part in the change.

Two key elements of leadership that support and drive change forward include engaging and empowering employees, as shown in Table 3.

Key terms

Employee engagement – When an organisation gets its employees interested and involved in their roles at work.

Employee empowerment – When employees are given the power to have greater influence over their role, e.g. by making decisions (within guidelines).

Absenteeism – Employees staying away from work without good reason. This is often more common during periods of change.

Examples of employee engagement	Examples of employee empowerment
Questionnaires to collect attitudes and opinions.	Employees making decisions within their clearly defined roles.
Regular meetings to get feedback.	Employees being able to give their opinions without worry in an open and constructive way.
Staff consultation groups to ask for ideas.	
Idea promotion competitions, e.g. suggestion schemes or groups.	Employees being able to be independent and being allowed to get on with their role.
Newsletters and briefings with updates.	Employees being aware of all the information affecting the organisation or the context of the change.
Breakfast briefings and lunches linked to opinion gathering.	
	Employees being accountable.

Table 3: Examples of engaging and empowering employees during change

Engaging and empowering employees tends to reduce **absenteeism**, too.

Organisation

Good leadership resulting in happy employees who are actively engaged and empowered in their roles means that change can happen effectively, but the change still needs to be organised properly. Tasks that are needed for change should take place in a timely way and within budget. Every time a change is delayed, it can have additional costs for resources or time. A motivated workforce ensures that the organisation continues to offer high quality and customers are not negatively affected during the change period.

Justification for change

Effective leaders need to explain why change is happening and justify the change, particularly if it is difficult. There are different types of change that you may encounter at work, shown in Table 4. It is important to consider the risks for the organisation of each change and the potential impact.

Change	Explanation and justification
Organisational restructure	Restructures take different forms but commonly affect middle managers or whole teams that can be put at risk of redundancy if savings need to be made.
Process	Process changes are often related to needing to do something differently. Process can also relate to storage or the way a service is offered.
Policy	Your organisation has many different policies and procedures that it uses. Sometimes these policies have to change because of a change in the law or because the organisation has to save costs or improve the way that it carries out its operations.
Technology	Technology advances very quickly. These changes may mean that what were manual tasks can now be automated.

Table 4: Different types of change

Key terms

Organisational restructure – When an organisation changes the number of employees that it requires within its structure or moves them to different areas of the organisation.

Resistance to change – When employees avoid a change or take steps to try to avoid a change happening.

Employees may be **resistant to change** because they are worried about how new procedures are going to affect them. It is important to engage them as much as possible with information on why the change is happening. Sometimes employees may lack faith in the process, so it is important for change leaders to meet them to hear their concerns.

Concerns raised during change commonly relate to employees potentially losing their jobs. This can be a very difficult time and cause stress and anxiety. Any negative reaction to change may disrupt operations, which could cause an organisation to lose money and impact on the organisation's future.

Requirements for managing change effectively (2)

You have already learned about the need to involve people and engage them in the process. Implementing change often needs the involvement of other stakeholder groups, such as staff consultation groups or trade unions.

Implementing change

It is important that if a change is likely to result in job changes or losses there is frequent and open communication about the change in order to try to reduce anxiety.

If change involving technology or new processes is underway, then support must be given by providing training to help employees prepare. Part of implementation is providing training in advance so that there is time for re-training and time to make adaptions if necessary.

Contingency planning when implementing change

We touched on contingency planning earlier in this chapter. Contingency planning means that back-up plans are available in case they are needed.

Organisations need to consider the risk of something happening as part of change and what should happen to reduce the impact if it does happen. There are also critical points in change, e.g. if something doesn't happen by a particular date then its impact will cause other parts of the plan to fail. You will learn more about the tools used to avoid this in the chapter on project management (Chapter 16).

It is also important that your organisation:

- plans for predictable events, which could involve allowing enough time, ensuring that there is sufficient finance available and that employees are available for work with the appropriate skills

- brings plans forward if conditions are positive, which means the change can happen earlier than expected, particularly if this benefits the organisation.

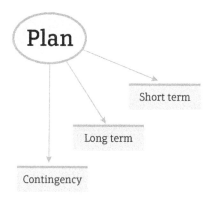

Figure 2: Think of a change that you will need to make and what could stop this change from happening. Write a contingency action for each of these negative outcomes.

Regularly evaluate and assess effectiveness during change implementation

Like financial planning, it is important with any change to keep comparing plans with what is actually happening. This can be checked through formal reports, questionnaires by managers checking the progress of the plans, or by less formal feedback such as chatting to employees involved in the process.

You should keep making judgements about the improvements being made and discuss any concerns with your line manager.

Adapt implementation of the change based on continuous review

Adapting plans and being flexible is important in all change management. When setting out on the journey of change there are often 'unknown unknowns' (things you did not even imagine happening) and changing the plans as soon as these become clear can avoid the whole change being disrupted.

Continuous review allows small changes in response to these events, avoiding larger problems developing. Strong leadership and good planning with effective monitoring can ensure change is a positive experience for all.

Key term

Continuous review – Constantly noting or checking progress, rather than doing it just once at a set time.

Impact of effective change management

Effective change management has a significant impact on the role of the administrator and on the whole organisation. Effective change management ensures that change is positive and that the organisation is strengthened by the change, not weakened by it.

Impact on administrator role

In your administration role there are two key ways that you can benefit from effective change management.

Identifies need for training

Some employees may view change anxiously but others may see it as an opportunity to progress and gain additional skills and knowledge.

Effective change management reviews your practice to decide what is working well but it also identifies areas for improvement. Once identified, you can target these gaps to get additional training to help you in your role.

Change in work procedures might also be as a result of new equipment or new technology. When this happens, it is important that you receive training to help you work effectively.

Whenever it happens, change management gives you an opportunity to review what you do, the skills that you have and your day-to-day performance.

Provides opportunities for promotion

Being trained and updated as part of effective change management also means that you can gain additional skills and qualifications. This can ultimately help you to a more highly paid and/or responsible role in your current organisation or in a new one.

What is your vision for your administration role over the next five years?

Impact on the organisation

As we have seen, effective change management affects individual employees as their levels of motivation and attitude fluctuate during a period of change. But managing change well is also important for the organisation. There are four key reasons for this, shown in Table 5.

Impact	Explanation
Increases competitiveness	During change, processes and procedures are reviewed to make them more efficient. New technology can also enable the organisation to offer new services or to be more efficient. All these aspects make organisations more **competitive** and this positively affects the organisation as it can offer new or improved services or products.
More effective/efficient performance	Effective change management will also positively affect employees, if they understand what is happening and can give their feedback. This means the work of the organisation is likely to become more effective as, for example, new technology, new teams or new locations are introduced. Reviewing performance also gives an opportunity to see if processes and ways of working are the most efficient. Sometimes you may have noticed that work is completed in a certain way because it has always been done that way, not necessarily because it is the best way of doing it. Effective change management gives an opportunity to review practice.
Ensures compliance with legislation or regulations	Sometimes it is new legislation that has brought the change about, for example health and safety legislation, data protection legislation or equality legislation (see Chapter 4). Being up to date with changes in law and regulations ensures that the organisation is not breaking the law. Being 'ahead of the game' and professional enhances the reputation of the organisation, which in turn should lead to higher numbers of customers or more satisfied stakeholders.
More likely to retain employees	Employees are more likely to be reassured and less likely to be anxious and leave if change is effectively managed. Retaining employees is cost effective because it avoids skills being lost and the need to give retraining to replacement staff.

Table 5: Key impacts of change on organisations

Key terms

Competitive – The organisation being as good as (or better than) its rivals and competitors so that customers or clients choose your organisation.

Project management principles

Project management principles help organisations ensure that change is managed effectively throughout the project life cycle. This will help the change project meet its **aims** and **objectives**.

You will learn more about the practical application and skills used to manage projects in Chapter 10, as you need to have knowledge of and be able to demonstrate your skills in project management as part of your apprenticeship. You will need to be clear about the stages of planning and managing a project and also the principles of project management and management tools.

These principles apply especially during change management. It is important that the project establishes timelines with appropriate deadlines to make sure that it keeps to schedule. If deadlines are not set, the timeline for the project may drift. It is also important that alerts are set up to flag up when deadlines are missed.

This primary planning stage is when **feasibility studies** are carried out to confirm whether the project should go ahead. It often results in **business cases** or **project proposals** having to be put forward to justify the project happening.

Impact of effective project management

Effective project management ensures that a change project is well planned, executed and reviewed. Effective project management can lead to organisations making the best use of employees' time and skills as well as making the most of unexpected opportunities. This has positive benefits for you in your role as administrator but also for your organisation, as success in a change project means that there is success overall.

Impact on administrator role

Having effective project management, whether that is you leading the project or being led by others, has three key benefits for you in your role.

Gives clear responsibilities and objectives in the project

Having clear responsibilities and objectives communicated to you and knowing what you and others are doing on the project means that you are more likely to feel motivated.

Makes you able to manage your time and resources

Effective project management also means that you will not spend time wondering what is expected of you. If you can make the best use of your time and resources, this will make you more efficient and productive, and therefore you will engage with the project more.

Using your time effectively also means that you are less likely to have to work additional hours. In addition, knowing what is expected means you can organise any equipment or other resources you need in advance.

Helps you to prioritise tasks

Effective project management ensures that you can consider priorities for the project against other routine work that you may be doing. If you know something needs to be completed in order to keep the project on time, then you can plan for this. This helps make you effective.

Impact on the organisation

As well as motivating and making individuals work efficiently, effective project management will have a positive impact on the organisation as new learning on one project can then be passed to another.

There are four key benefits of effective management for your organisation.

Identifies and gives opportunity to adapt to unexpected situations

During any project you will find that new opportunities or unexpected events happen. Effective management takes these unexpected situations and turns them into positives. If something happens that was not planned, it is the way that leaders and managers use that information that will lead to a positive outcome.

Enables successful resolution of unexpected risks or problems

During any project, there will always be problems that were not expected. Reacting to unexpected situations by using contingency plans, adding further control measures or even revising the plan will ensure that the situation is resolved, and risks are removed or their impact reduced, so that the project is not negatively affected.

Sometimes these situations may occur as a result of an accident or incident and because the delivery of the project significantly changes. Making alternative arrangements or communicating with stakeholders to avoid problems is important.

Develops project management 'best practice'

The more that effective and efficient project management techniques, tools and ways of working are detailed and shared, the more likely your organisation is to meet the aims of any change project it undertakes. This can include increasing the chances of the project being on time and without additional cost and reworking, which requires extra effort. Effective tools ensure that effective management leads to great results.

Allows operational improvements to be made

Effective project management also gives the organisation an opportunity to review its operations and to make suggestions and improvements more widely. Bringing employees together to work on projects helps to share understanding. This leads to **operational improvements** for the whole organisation and improved motivation for the whole workforce.

Key term

Operational improvements – Improvements to any aspect of the day-to-day running or operations of the organisation.

Summary

In this section you have learned about the relevance of business principles. It has covered:
- principles of business finance relevant to the administrative role
- the impact of following financial processes on both your role and the organisation
- the principles of managing change
- the impact of effective change management on both your role and the organisation
- the impact of effective project management on both your role and the organisation.

Activities

▶ Activity 1: National Insurance (NI)

The government website (www.gov.uk) provides useful information for employers on how to calculate National Insurance (NI).

Access the website and review how NI is calculated. Make notes.

▶ Activity 2: Budgeting

Review your own budgets if you are a budget holder or talk to your line manager about the different ways that budgets are used in your organisation.

- Do you use allocated or zero based budgeting? How are the budgets negotiated? How are they recorded?
- Are there ways that budgeting could be improved to make it even more accurate or is it perfect already?

▶ Activity 3: Efficient financial processes

How efficient are the financial processes at your organisation?

How often do you have to chase others for information or repeat work because financial data has changed or been lost?

Could the financial processes be updated to be more efficient?

Write three recommendations for improvement and discuss these with your line manager.

▶ Activity 4: Security breach

You have learned in this chapter about the importance of securing data. Carry out an emergency planning review of what would happen in your organisation if there was a security breach related to personal data: how would this be managed, who would take control, are there any further steps that could be avoided?

▶ Activity 5: Change at work

Using Kotter's steps for change, think of a change that you have experienced at work. What happened and why?

How many of the steps did your organisation follow when communicating the change?

What happened after the change took place?

▶ Activity 6: Changing technology

Technology is changing very rapidly and therefore the way that it is used at work changes too. Think back to the first mobile phone that you owned or used.

- How does it compare to what you have today?
- How does this change in technology affect how you work?
- How was that planned for?

▶ Activity 7: Cover for your administration role

- Do you have a contingency plan for who would cover your work if you were seconded to do another role for three months?
- Could your role be covered?
- Who knows what you do if you were not there?

Discuss your findings with your line manager. If you find any gaps in the cover that could be provided, work out a contingency plan for the future.

▶ Activity 8: Changes in my organisation

Draw up a table showing change that has happened in your organisation using the four headings of *Restructure*, *Process*, *Policy* and *Technology*.

Under each heading write the change that has happened and why.

If you are new to your organisation, talk to your line manager or co-workers about changes that have happened.

Consider the nature of the change and the justification of those changes. How have they worked out and why?

▶ Activity 9: Contingency planning

Think of a change that you will need to make in the way you work over the next 12 months. It could be a small or large change.

Now think of all the possible elements that could stop this change happening. For each one write a contingency action demonstrating what you would do if any of these negative outcomes happened.

Share your ideas with your line manager.

▶ Activity 10: Administration role planning

What is your vision for your administration role over the next five years?

You will have completed your Level 3 Business Administrator Apprenticeship but what are your plans for the future? What changes are likely to happen in your organisation and how can you prepare yourself for promotion through training and professional working?

Review your own performance and write a list of areas that you should consider.

Discuss your ideas with your line manager during appraisal or professional review.

Topic consolidation

▶ Test yourself

1. **Financial processes**
   - ☐ I am aware of the four key types of financial process relevant to administrators.
   - ☐ I can describe each of the types.
   - ☐ I can give examples of the type of financial processes used in my organisation.
   - ☐ I need to review my understanding of financial processes at my organisation and more generally.

2. **Impact of financial processes**
   - ☐ I am clear about the impact of effective financial processes on my administrative role.
   - ☐ I can describe the impact of effective financial processes on my organisation.
   - ☐ I understand what is meant by compliance with relevant legislation and regulations for financial processes.
   - ☐ I need to find out more about effective financial processes and how they apply to my role and my organisation more generally.

3. **Managing change**
   - ☐ I can describe the different types of change, giving examples for step, incremental, planned and unplanned change.
   - ☐ I can give judgements about the requirements for leadership in managing change effectively.
   - ☐ I know the difference between the impact of organisational restructure and technological change when assessing business risks for change.
   - ☐ I am not clear about managing change, including the different types, justifications and ways of implementing change.

4. **Effective change management**
   - ☐ I know how identifying training needs can support effective change management, including how it is applied.
   - ☐ I am clear how effective change management can lead to opportunities for promotion and can describe how this can happen.
   - ☐ I can describe how effective change management leads to increased organisational competitiveness.
   - ☐ I am not clear about what is meant by effective change management.

5. **Project life cycle**
   - ☐ I have a clear understanding of the different stages of the project life cycle.
   - ☐ I understand how the project life cycle can help my organisation.
   - ☐ I have a very good understanding of the application and limitations of the product life cycle for my organisation and my role.
   - ☐ I need to find out more the project life cycle.

6. **Effective project management**
   - ☐ I can list three impacts of effective project management on my administrator role.
   - ☐ I can describe four impacts of effective project management on my organisation.
   - ☐ I know what is meant by operational improvements.
   - ☐ I am clear about the impact of effective project management on meeting project aims and objectives.

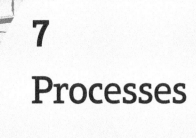

7

Processes

Processes

It is important that you understand the processes that help your organisation operate, such as processing customer data and administering invoices or purchase orders. You need to be able to demonstrate that you:

- understand and consistently follow your organisation's processes
- can make suggestions for small improvements in processes and support their successful implementation.

Following and promoting organisational processes

Your organisation will use its own processes to make sure that day-to-day work is carried out in a particular way. You need to show that you effectively follow and promote your organisation's processes.

Processes at work are like sets of instructions for employees that say how to carry out their work. Having a common set of instructions ensures that employees are clear about what they need to do and how they need to do it, and ensures consistency across the organisation. They clarify each step in a situation.

Processes should be as clear and as short as possible so that they are accessible by everyone. If a process is unclear or instructions are not provided, it may mean an employee gets something wrong. This could negatively affect the organisation. Processes can cover many different areas, such as those shown in Table 1. If an employee does not follow a process, then disciplinary action may be taken or expenses owed to the employee might not be paid.

Process area	Example
Purchasing	Credit/debit card use (both online and offline) Processing statements and receipts when using credit card Handling petty cash, cash payments and receipts Administering billing Processing invoices and purchase orders
Travel and subsistence	Purchasing travel tickets and booking hire cars Claims for mileage and subsistence amounts for meals Booking overnight accommodation
Customer service	Communicating by telephone and email Taking orders Dealing with complaints or compliments Handling refunds
Bookings and meetings	Booking rooms/meetings Producing meeting minutes (including using template and distribution or circulation lists)

Table 1: Common types of processes

With any process, it is important that you remind your colleagues to use it and are positive about its use. Remind them why processes are helpful to follow.

Suggesting improvements in your organisation's processes

Your organisation will have many different processes in operation for all sorts of different purposes, including those that relate to equipment and building maintenance, adverse weather conditions, selling used equipment and retaining records. All are vital for the smooth working of the organisation. If there is a concern about a process, or a process seems lacking, it is important that you make suggestions for improvement and help the organisation be even more efficient.

Most of the time you will have comprehensive processes to follow that will adequately guide you in what you need to do. However, other times there may be missing information or the information may be unclear. If this is the case, you should suggest to your line manager how that process could be improved. The aim is always to make the process more efficient and/or effective – see Table 2.

Efficient	Getting more or better work out of following the process, with the least amount of effort or money being wasted on stages that are not necessary or are expensive. An efficient process avoids waste.
Effective	Making a process have the best possible result with the fewest errors yet making the process as simple as possible or making sure it involves the least amount of re-working that is possible after the process has been carried out.

Table 2: The aim of efficient and effective processes

Behaviours

Responsibility – Demonstrates taking responsibility for team performance and quality of projects delivered. Takes a clear interest in seeing that projects are successfully completed and customer requests handled appropriately. Takes initiative to develop own and others' skills and behaviours.

Identifying and solving inefficiencies and ineffectiveness in a process is crucial. It means that your organisation can benefit in many ways. It:

- saves time as processes are carried out more quickly
- avoids having to repeat tasks due to errors
- reduces double checks if the process is carried out more quickly and correctly
- makes the process easier to follow if unnecessary steps are removed
- reduces overall administration, so more work can be completed
- uses fewer resources, such as less paper or repeated information
- is more secure because information is only being used for a specific purpose.

Summary

In this section you have learned about how to develop your understanding of your organisation's processes. It has covered:
- how to review processes and make suggestions for improvement
- how to improve business processes.

Activities

▶ Activity 1: Understanding and following a process

Find an organisational process that you do not follow, asking your line manager to guide you on the most appropriate process to help you in your role.

Go through each of the stages in the process, noting where the information is clear and where you have any questions. Note these down on a copy of the process.

Add the process that has your notes on it to your folder and discuss your findings with your line manager.

▶ Activity 2: Writing a process document

Think of a process that you carry out at work that does not currently have a written process.

Write a document detailing each of the stages and print a copy for your file.

Ask your colleagues for feedback on the process you have created, how you have written it and ways it could be improved. Make notes of their feedback and add it to your portfolio.

Write a final draft of your process for approval by your line manager and, once approved, add this to your portfolio too.

Having effective processes will help any organisation function much more efficiently.

▶ Activity 3: Making a process more efficient and effective

Think of a process that you regularly use but that you have not reviewed in your portfolio so far.

Review the way that the process is carried out. Are there any stages that could be reduced to make the process faster? What is the impact of each of the stages of the process? Could they be more effective?

Note for each of the stages whether it could be improved (or not) and suggest where they could be more efficient and effective.

Discuss with your line manager and ask for feedback on your ideas.

Write a statement outlining the positive benefit of your suggested changes and the timescales for your suggestions to be implemented, for approval by your line manager.

At a suitable time after the process has been implemented (e.g. a week or a month), review the process's implementation. Add a follow-up statement to your portfolio showing your successful change.

▶ Activity 4: Reviewing an existing organisational process

Find a process that exists in your organisation, for example the way to claim travel or subsistence.

Review how the process works and how easy it is to follow.

What are the strengths of this process?

What could be improved about this process?

Now rewrite the process using changes that you would recommend.

Take the original and new draft policy and discuss the differences and improvements with your line manager.

Put both copies in your portfolio ready for discussion.

▶ Activity 5: Comparing organisational processes

Find a common process that is being used in your organisation and one that you think would be common in other organsiations similar to yours.

Carry out research or email other employees in these similar organisations (make sure you check with your line manager that they are happy for you to contact these organisations).

Contrast and compare the processes and write a set of bullet points with recommendations between the two about how each can be improved.

Now add the two processes with your thoughts to your portfolio for discussion.

Topic consolidation

▶ Test yourself

1. A subsistence claim process at work helps employees to be clear about:
   - ☐ purchase order processing.
   - ☐ meal allowances that can be claimed.
   - ☐ purchasing of train tickets.
   - ☐ how to work with customers.

2. Processes should be kept:
   - ☐ as long as possible.
   - ☐ as detailed as possible.
   - ☐ as simple as possible.
   - ☐ as complicated as possible.

3. Customer service processes include guidance for:
   - ☐ purchasing travel claims.
   - ☐ booking rooms for meetings.
   - ☐ speaking to customers by telephone or on paper.
   - ☐ processing bank statements.

4. Promoting the use of processes means:
   - ☐ following processes that are in place.
   - ☐ making up new processes.
   - ☐ encouraging others to follow established processes.
   - ☐ ignoring established processes.

5. Efficient processes are those that are best described as:
   - ☐ using the most effort and least amount of waste to get the best result.
   - ☐ using the least amount of effort and least amount of waste to get the best result.
   - ☐ using the least amount of effort and most resources to get the best result.
   - ☐ using the most effort and the most resources to get the best result.

6. Effective processes are those that are best described as:
   - ☐ using a complex method to get the best possible result.
   - ☐ using the simplest method to get the most defective result.
   - ☐ using the simplest method to get the best possible result.
   - ☐ using a complex method to get the most defective result.

7. Two benefits of having effective and efficient processes are:
   - ☐ less double checking and reworking.
   - ☐ increasing resources and making the organisation less secure.
   - ☐ saving time and avoiding repetition.
   - ☐ increasing administration and greater complexity.

8

External factors

External factors

There are a huge number of different factors that affect the way you work and your organisation. You need to be aware of external factors that affect not just your day-to-day role but also the future of your organisation and be able to explain how your organisation is affected. This ties in with what you looked at in Chapter 1. You need to be aware of seven factors:

- political and economic factors
- social and technological factors
- legal and environmental factors
- market forces.

Political factors (1)

Political factors affect organisations because changes in government, monetary policy and fiscal policy all influence the way that organisations operate, the amount of tax that they pay and the value of money.

Changes in government

Government changes have a big impact on the way that organisations carry out their activities. This in turn has an impact on your administrative role. The UK government is led by a **prime minister** who operates from 10 Downing Street. Changes in government often lead to changes in policy and relationships with other countries.

Style and degree of government intervention

The style of government is set by the party that is in power. Different parties have different views on the way that the country should be run. The government in the UK is formed by the party that gets the most votes in a **general election** or, if no single party has enough MPs, a 'coalition government' of two or more parties may be formed. For example, in June 2017 the general election gave the Conservative Party the most votes across the country as a whole but it did not have more than half the MPs in parliament. This meant it could not pass laws without the other parties agreeing to them. To help avoid this, the Conservative government signed an agreement with the Democratic Unionist Party (DUP) so that they did have more than half of the votes.

In recent times, the two largest parties with MPs in the House of Commons and therefore the biggest influence have been the Conservative and Labour parties. Their politics are different (see Table 1), although they sometimes strongly agree (or disagree!) with each other's thinking on different aspects of policy.

Party	Style and approach to intervention
Conservative	Focus on private ownership and enterprise (the **private sector**)
	Investment in the military
	Increasing private companies' investment in services, rather than state intervention, to help economic prosperity, reduce inequality and keep taxes lower
Labour	Focus on the state helping to create economic prosperity
	Traditional focus on socialism and the working classes with historic links to trade unions
	Support for higher taxation to tackle poverty and inequality

Table 1: Different approaches of the main political parties

International relations

Changes in government also affect the UK's attitude towards working with other countries and **international relations**. Although you may think this would not affect your administrative role at work, it does influence what is happening in the wider context of the UK and, therefore, your organisation.

For example, the government's changing attitudes towards different countries can have a significant influence as organisations are affected by:

- negotiated international trade deals
- investment in technology and the opening or closing of factories by investors from overseas
- visits by members of the UK government to different countries
- visits to the UK by leaders and representatives of governments from other states to discuss sharing information or policies
- investment in military spending, for example for security, or by sending troops to other countries to help in wars or other emergencies.

If the UK government changes the way it works with countries, for example by introducing **trade tariffs**, then this can make the price of goods coming into the UK more expensive. It can also mean that products from your organisation have additional taxes on them when they are sold into another country. If two countries do not have good international relations, this can lead to a **trade war** which could affect the supply of goods or services between the countries and prices.

In June 2016 the UK voted to leave the European Union. This will have an impact on the way that goods are exported from and imported into the UK, with the possibility of additional tariffs and changes to the cost of goods for customers.

Have the changes in the UK affected your organisation's trade?

Having good international relations also helps the UK share expertise between countries so, if your organisation is involved in research or activities across the world, good international relations may mean that good practice can be shared.

Political factors (2)

Key term

Monetary policy – The process that the Bank of England uses to control the UK economy, such as setting the base rate from which all other interest rates are set.

Changes in monetary policy

Monetary policy is the way that a country controls the supply of money circulating in the economy. In the UK it is set by the Bank of England, which was established in 1694. Although the Bank of England sets monetary policy independently, it is owned by the UK government and still counts as a political factor.

The Monetary Policy Committee (MPC) of the Bank of England makes decisions about whether or not it needs to increase or restrict the supply of money in the UK. It does this by increasing or reducing the supply of coins and bank notes circulating in the economy and by changing the rate of interest that it offers to other banks and building societies.

The Bank of England has targets that it tries to achieve by using monetary policy. These include trying to make sure that inflation is at a certain level and influencing whether the UK's economy grows or shrinks.

The Bank of England's interest rate has a big impact on your organisation and you too if you have a mortgage or other borrowing. This is because the Bank of England's 'base rate' influences the borrowing of all other financial institutions in the UK economy. The higher the Bank of England base rate is set at, the more money you will need to pay in interest on borrowing. However, if you have savings, you will receive more interest.

Find out more about the role of the Bank of England and the work it does. Its website is a good starting point.

As well as changing its interest rate, the Bank of England can help to make the economy grow or shrink by using **quantitative easing**. This puts money into the economy. Sometimes people call this 'printing more money' but money is not actually printed; it is digitally created and then used to buy assets within the economy (such as stocks, shares or money borrowed from other banks).

Rise or fall in inflation

The Bank of England has a target to make sure that the UK economy is healthy and sustainable and one of the ways of measuring this is inflation. Inflation is the rate of increase in the price of goods and services in the UK. It is shown as a percentage (%) – if inflation is 1% then prices are 1% higher than they were a year ago.

Inflation is worked out by the Bank of England using the **consumer price index (CPI)**. If the increase in inflation is too high, the bank will act to try to reduce the amount people spend by increasing the Bank of England base interest rate. When this happens, individuals and organisations have less money to spend so demand goes down.

Calculating percentages

There are various ways to calculate percentages but the following worked examples are a reminder of one of them.

If a watch cost £100 a year ago and it now costs £103, its price has increased by £3.

- £3 divided by £100 = 0.03
- × 100 for the percentage = 3%

If a computer cost £565 last year and now costs £572, its price has increased by £7

- £7 divided by £565 = 0.012
- × 100 for percentage = 1.2%

To work out the potential increase of a watch, you can multiply its current price by the rate of inflation that you think will apply to work out the approximate expected price. This is only a prediction but can help with budgeting. (When using a calculator, press the % key rather than the = key to get the total!)

- If a watch costs £100 now and the rate of inflation is 2.5%, in a year the watch will cost £100 × 102.5% = £102.50
- If a computer costs £565 and the rate of inflation is 2.5%, in a year the computer will cost £565 × 102.5% = £579.13

Increase or decrease in economic growth

The economy is measured by **gross domestic product (GDP)** and this measure is also used by the Bank of England to work out whether or not interest rates need to be increased or decreased.

If the economy is growing too quickly and inflation is getting higher than it would like, the Bank of England may choose to increase the base rate. This will make costs go up, which is likely to reduce the growth in the economy and bring inflation down.

If economic growth comparing one quarter or year with the previous one is decreasing, the Bank of England may choose to lower its base rate and undertake quantitative easing to stimulate the economy.

Key terms

Quantitive easing – When the Bank of England starts to buy assets from other organisations such as banks to help grow the economy.

Consumer price index (CPI) – A measure that looks at the price of all items that we spend money on, including food, clothing and entertainment, but which does not include the amount we spend on housing and mortgages.

Gross domestic product (GDP) – The value of all the goods and services produced within a certain time period (often a quarter or year) by individuals and organisations. It is possible to compare the GDP for different countries.

Political factors (3)

Key terms

Fiscal policy – The amount of money that the government spends or receives in taxes that it uses to help grow or shrink the economy.

Public services or **public sector** – Services that are organised by the government to help the community, such as healthcare, colleges, the police and road maintenance.

Changes in fiscal policy

The **fiscal policy** of the government affects the amount of money that is taken from the economy or put back into it. There are two ways that this happens: through taxes (taking money from the economy) and through the amount that is spent by government on **public services** (putting money back into it).

Changes to levels of taxation

The amount of money that is taken in taxes by the government affects the amount of money that is available in the economy. This impacts organisations in two ways.

1) The amount of tax the organisation has to pay

Tax that is paid by organisations affects them in many different ways.

Most organisations have to pay tax on their annual profits (the amount of money that they make at the end of the year). This is called corporation tax. The amount of tax paid depends on the amount of profit the organisation makes.

Organisations also have to pay tax on products and services that they buy, known as value added tax (VAT). The level of VAT depends on the type of goods or services being paid for and whether or not the organisation, such as charities or schools, can claim the money back. If VAT increases, then the organisation has to pay more to HM Revenue & Customs and this means that the organisation has less money to spend elsewhere.

Organisations using transport are affected by other types of taxes. For example, if they run a fleet of company cars, they have to pay tax on insurance premiums, vehicle excise duty (based on how much the vehicle pollutes the environment) and tax on fuel. If there is an increase in any of those taxes, this will affect the organisation and how much it needs to pay.

All employees must pay a form of tax called National Insurance (NI). NI pays for state-provided pensions, sickness benefits and so on. When an employee pays this insurance, their employer also has to pay a sum of additional NI on their behalf. The amount that is paid depends on the amount that the employee earns. The amount of NI the employer needs to pay changes if National Insurance levels change.

2) The amount of tax that customers are paying

The amount of tax that individuals have to pay also affects your organisation. If customers have got more money in their pockets then they are more likely to be able to spend money on goods and services – the goods and services that organisations like yours produce. If they have less money, they won't be able to spend so much.

If your organisation offers non-essential luxury goods or services, it is more likely to be affected by changes in disposable income than an organisation that offers something essential to everyday living, which customers still have to buy regardless of its price.

Changes to levels of government spending

Government spending also affects your organisation.

The government can increase spending within their own organisations (the public sector). This could be done, for example, by giving more money to local councils for them to spend or by increasing staffing levels within the public sector in an attempt to improve services.

Alternatively, the government can increase spending in the private sector. Examples of private sector spending or investment include:

- road building
- house building
- buying defence equipment, such as military planes or ships
- private prisons and security firms
- private training providers
- private research organisations.

Governments contract different private organisations to offer investment in these areas and then the private organisations undertake the work. This might involve building new facilities such as prisons, or running facilities, or both. The private organisations are usually profit making, unlike the public sector. The work undertaken by the private organisations can be very specialist.

How has your organisation been directly or indirectly affected by government spending?

When there is a rise in government spending, there is usually an increase in economic growth because there is more demand as more activity is happening.

When there is a fall in government spending, there is usually a decrease in economic growth because there is less demand as less activity is happening.

Each UK government has its own philosophy and attitude towards spending – some are more in favour of it than others.

Economic factors – working population and skills

You have already learned about how political factors affect the economy but there are further economic factors which also affect it. One of the biggest relates to the **labour market**: to the working population, their skills and how much it costs to employ them.

Changes in the labour market

Labour is the supply of people who are available for work. This means the number of people who can and are able to work – 'the working population'. It does not include those in the UK who cannot work for reasons such as ill health or old age.

The supply of people in the UK has a big impact on organisations and on you as an employee. The supply of current and potential workers can affect whether your organisation works effectively: if people leave your organisation for a new job or retire, they need to be replaced! The labour market is significantly affected by three factors: the working population, their skills and increases or decreases in costs.

The working population

The working population is made up of every person above the age of 15 who is willing and eligible to work. This population is important because not only can they work for organisations, but if they do so they will also pay taxes which go to the government.

There are lots of ways of measuring the number of people in work and this data is published every quarter by the **Office for National Statistics (ONS)**. In May 2018, it showed that the employment rate in the UK was the highest it had been since records began in 1971.

When the employment rate is high, it usually means that there are fewer people available for work and therefore employers need to pay more to their employees to make sure they stay at their organisation.

When the employment rate is lower it means that organisations may find it easier to source new employees and they may be less likely to pay higher wages to retain staff. This will depend on the type of work the organisation does and where it is located. In some areas of the UK it is more challenging to recruit people.

This leads to supply and demand in the labour market, with the number of people who are available being the supply and demand coming from the number of organisations that want to employ them.

The working population is also affected by the number of people entering the workforce as they finish education, the number of people coming to the UK from other countries and the number of people taking retirement. This means that the birth rate in the UK affects the number of young people who become available for work in a given year.

Key terms

Labour market – The number of people who are available for work in an economy and the number of organisations that are wanting people to work for them.

Office for National Statistics (ONS) – The body that produces official statistics for the UK.

The UK birth rate was high in the 1960s but has reduced and now remains much lower in comparison. This means that the number of people born in the 1960s who are in the workforce is likely to be higher than those born in the 1990s, for example. This affects the working population as fewer people of a working age means there are fewer people to fill jobs.

The working population is also affected by citizens coming to the UK for work from overseas. The number available for work can influence the variety of skills on offer and the number of employers that are looking for employees.

The last group that affects the overall number is those people who have nearly reached retirement. Retirement age in the UK used to be 60 for women and 65 for men. However, this 'default retirement age' no longer exists. This means older workers can continue past 65 if they wish and some workers cannot claim state or work-related pensions until they are 67 or 68, unless their job has an age limit, for example a fire officer.

Skills shortages

Skills shortages also affect organisations where highly skilled workers are needed to carry out activities. If there are not enough people with the right qualifications, then work may not be completed. In this situation, potential employees can demand high salaries, reflecting the increased demand for their skills.

Skills shortages occur if there are not enough employers paying for training or if too few people want to do the work on offer. Skills shortages can be reduced by:

- investing in training such as apprenticeships
- recruiting fewer experienced employees, instead 'training up' inexperienced people
- improving careers education to encourage more people to go to college or university to continue their education
- encouraging skilled staff to transfer sectors or move to different stages in the same sector.

What training could you do after your apprenticeship to improve your skills?

Behaviours B

Managing performance – Takes responsibility for their own work, accepts feedback in a positive way, uses initiative and shows resilience. Also takes responsibility for their own development, knows when to ask questions to complete a task and informs their line manager when a task is complete. Performs thorough self-assessments of their work and complies with the organisation's procedures.

Economic factors – costs

You have learned about the economic impact on your organisation and your own role of the working population and skills shortages. However, there is one final external economic factor that has a big impact on the organisation and its behaviour. This relates to costs and whether they are increasing or decreasing.

Increases or decreases in costs

All costs affect the way that your organisation operates. A cost can make the difference between whether or not an organisation that aims to make a profit does so; if the organisation is a charity or a publicly funded organisation, it may affect their ability to **break-even** or make a surplus to be reinvested back into the organisation.

There are many different costs organisations have to meet, so the extent to which these costs increase or decrease affects the overall financial position of the organisation. Some of the types of cost that organisations face are shown in Table 2.

Oil is a raw material that has a big impact on manufacturing and the supply chain.

Cost	Impact of an increase or decrease
Raw materials	If materials are scarce then the cost of them goes up. It will cost the organisation more money to make its products or provide its services. You will learn more about this later in this chapter (in the section on market forces) but essentially the more that raw materials are wanted, the higher the price that must be paid. The opposite applies if there are too many.
Products	Products themselves can go up or down in price due to many factors. This can have an impact on the organisation regardless of whether the product is used as a component of what the organisation sells or whether it uses the product in its day-to-day activities, such as ink for a printer.
Supply chain	The **supply chain** can affect all elements of the delivery of the product or service. This covers increased costs during manufacturing the product, for example due to increases in electricity costs or skills shortages, through to reductions in costs when companies merge or work together to get bigger **economies of scale**.
Services	Services that are used by the organisation can include anything from routine health and safety checks through to additional training or guidance from consultants.
Staff	You have learned a lot about staff already. The impact of not having enough people available to recruit and the impact of not having enough qualified people in the organisation don't just stop the organisation from running efficiently and operating at the best possible level – they also mean extra costs for extra training and recruitment.

Table 2: Types of cost faced by organisations

Key terms

Supply chain – All the organisations and people directly or indirectly that help make a product or service and deliver it to the customer. It covers everything from components being produced to getting it to the final customer, e.g. the parcel delivery company that ships a parcel from the manufacturer to the customer.

Economies of scale – Being able to pay a cheaper price for something because it is bought in bulk.

Social factors – trends and behaviours

Social factors are those trends and changes that affect the way **society** behaves. This can present organisations with challenges but also opportunities.

Changes in trends

You will be aware of changes in the way that you and your friends might behave based on what is popular or in fashion at a given time. Fashion changes frequently and there are different trends that people follow. The result of this is that demand for a particular product or service offered may increase – or it may decrease, presenting the organisation with a challenge. You will need to be aware of the way that changes in trends affect you and your organisation.

Society's behaviours

The way that people behave is affected by the expectations or trends in behaviour. 'Society' can refer to the entire UK population, to part of the UK (for example Wales) or within a county such as North Yorkshire. The way that groups of people behave in those groups is influenced by lots of different factors, shown in Table 3.

Influence	How this affects society's behaviours and the organisation
Media	The media (TV, film, etc.) affects consumer demand for products or services and perceptions about those products. A trend in wanting to do something can create a high demand but, if the trend changes and interest falls, an organisation can find itself without customers. Organisations offering toys or services for children can be greatly affected by such changes, for example at Christmas when demand gets so high that there may be too few products available, creating a 'must have' item that can sell for more than it was originally priced.
Crime	The level of crime can influence the extent to which people are involved in activities, the protection they give to their homes and how people behave, for example whether or not they choose to take drugs or steal. Crime also has an impact on the organisation and its employees as it increases costs such as insurance, while encouraging people to buy safety and security equipment such as alarms.
Education	The level of education of a society affects how that group of people behave and the type of products or lifestyles desired in that area. It tends to be that, where the level of education in a society is higher, the population demonstrates more healthy behaviours and this influences the type of products and services offered by organisations.
Family and work	Organisations are affected by who goes out to work in a family, who purchases products for the home, the number of hours that are being worked each week, holiday that is being taken and absence from work such as illness.

Table 3: Influences on society

Beliefs

Your organisation is also affected by the **beliefs** held by different groups and society as a whole. Beliefs include religious beliefs: the largest religion in the UK is Christianity, followed by Islam. However, the number of people who report they do not have a religious belief has been increasing.

Beliefs affect organisations as they influence the type of products that are bought, for example products with links to religious festivals such as Christmas, Eid or Diwali. There may be increased purchasing of goods and services at these times or requests for changes to holidays or working patterns of staff for celebrations. Working days of the week and working hours may also be different.

Level and awareness of social responsibility

Your organisation will have an impact on others in the way that it carries out its activities and the community in and around

Days for the weekend differ across the world. Find out which days are used overseas and consider the impact on your organisation if you were working with these countries.

it. Your individual awareness of **social responsibility** and that of your organisation are important because they determine how you affect others. Social responsibility considers all welfare and environmental impacts but common themes include:

- recycling – how you recycle, the materials purchased, e.g. whether or not recyclable, and the amount the organisation seeks to reduce waste

- looking after the wider environment – cleaning up in and around the local area, for example, to remove packaging or advertising material

- giving money to local worthwhile causes and charities

- giving time to raise awareness of supporting causes, such as donating time to help with education, supporting work experience, etc.

- enhancing sustainability, for example by helping suppliers by investing in them to encourage them to develop good environmental practices.

Social factors – demographics

The profile of a society has a big impact on your organisation. This is because it affects the type of people who are interested in your products or services and, as you have already learned, the workforce that is available. There are five key **demographic** changes that influence your organisation.

Income

The amount of household income that individuals have affects the amount that they have available to spend. In turn, this affects demand for the goods or services that your organisation has on offer.

Income is measured nationally by **household income**. If household incomes are increasing then there is more likely to be money to spare for luxuries. If it is going down then this is less likely. Disposable income across society is also affected by the balance between those people in and out of work, such as those in retirement.

In 2018, the average income was going up, meaning that the disposable incomes of retired people were most commonly increasing. This does not mean everyone's income was increasing, but that it was increasing for the most common average group.

Gender

The number of men and women in a society and their needs or wants also affects your organisation and how it behaves. This may be on a regional or national basis.

In the UK, the number of men and women in the population are almost equal. In 2017, the population was 51 per cent female compared with 49 per cent male.

Class

Class affects your organisation as goods or services may be targeted at different groups. This targeting can be based on earnings, education, family links or lifestyles that have been developed from the person's upbringing or wealth.

The influence of class may depend on the area where your organisation is based and how widely required your goods or services are. However, sociologists continually review this work and, in the UK, there is a suggestion that we have a 'classless' society.

Age

The UK population is continuing to grow, and the number of people aged 65 and over is now 18 per cent of the total population. This has an effect on your organisation as the changing age profile impacts on products and services that your organisation may offer or the availability of the workforce.

The distribution of older people in the UK is not the same in all areas. The Office for National Statistics (ONS) has projected the impact of this changing profile up to the year 2036. By then, it is expected that 30 per cent of the population in areas such as Great Yarmouth will be aged 65 or over, whereas in Southwark in London it will be 12 per cent of the population.

Are people in your local community for each demographic group increasing or decreasing?

Ethnicity

Ethnicity is the group within which people have common identities. This might be a common heritage, culture, language, religion or other factor. In different parts of the UK the ethnic make-up is very different and this affects the type of services or goods that may be demanded by the local community.

If the number of people from a particular ethnic group is increasing or decreasing, then demand is likely to be affected. Organisations should understand the ethnic profile of their area to help them grow.

Technological factors (1)

Technological factors are those that affect the way that your organisation carries out its operations and how you perform your role. Staying up to date with technology is important so that your organisation can remain competitive or provide the most effective services.

Changes in technology

The pace of technological change is very fast. You and your organisation need to keep up to date and continually plan for the next steps to enable you to support your customers and ensure that you are as efficient as possible.

Mobile technologies

Mobile technology has significantly changed over the past ten years, particularly in the way that we interact with each other and with our customers. Keeping administration up to date and the methods and technologies for supporting this are crucial.

Mobile phones have changed so significantly that they have moved away from just being devices used for text messaging and calls. Smartphones are capable of performing all the functions that traditionally would have taken place in an office: video calling, emailing, attaching files, voice transcription, photography and video, and much more.

Key term

4G – Broadband networks which are present in the UK to link mobile devices. The 'next generation' will be 5G.

Laptops and tablets have also become smaller and can now be used as multifunctional devices that can be linked to Wi-Fi and used anywhere in the organisation, or when travelling. The biggest barrier to mobile technology is now the availability of connections and the quality of those connections, such as Wi-Fi and broadband network technology and **4G** or 5G.

Software developments

Software is always being updated. It is vital that you know and understand the latest versions of the software that you use and their capabilities. Software developments also mean that it is possible to access software from different locations using different devices.

Many organisations now have computer servers that allow authorised users to connect to the system from anywhere in the world. These users do not need specific software installed on their own machines as they can operate 'in the cloud' over the internet.

Software developments are summarised in Table 4.

Developments in software	Impact on the organisation and administration role
Email	Email is accessible, personalised and increasingly essential. It can be used not just for communication within your organisation but for communicating with customers and other stakeholders. Most email software can track whether emails have been opened, the time they were opened and then what customers did next. This provides important information for organisations to follow up, helping to ensure that the customer experience is positive and that customers return.
Office applications	Office applications cover all the software packages that you might use in your organisation, including word processing, spreadsheets and databases. You may have specific software that your organisation uses and this may be regularly updated or changed depending on the needs of the organisation. Keeping up to date with the latest versions of software and making sure that they can offer new features is important. If organisations don't keep up to date with their customers, those organisations are less likely to retain their customers and this could affect the organisation's future success.
Management information systems (MIS)	Management information systems are used for a variety of reasons. They provide 'back end' functions to organisations, such as process control systems, accounting and finance systems, and **inventory** control systems. They may be **bespoke** or bought from other organisations. Developments in this area mean that access to these systems is frequently available 24/7 and from a variety of locations. Customers also want 24/7 access and the organisation may never really be closed as orders can be placed and tracked at any time. MIS information can also predict consumer patterns which can be used to help plan future marketing. It is important for the organisation to ensure that there are staff who can maintain the systems and operate them effectively.

Table 4: Software developments

Key terms

Inventory – The amount of a product that an organisation has in stock.

Bespoke – Systems or software that have been designed specifically for an organisation, commonly designed and maintained by IT staff.

Electronic point of sale systems

Electronic point of sale systems (EPOS) are increasingly in use. These are the cash register tills that are connected to the organisation's IT network. They provide many benefits.

- Barcodes mean fewer errors are made when keying in information, for example in a retail environment into a till.

- Customers can use self-service facilities, for example collecting pre-ordered tickets at a train station or at the cinema.

- Trends can be spotted immediately, for example spikes in sales or the number of days in service.

Technological factors (2)

Video conferencing

Video conferencing has had a major influence on the way that organisations operate. Instead of having to send people overseas or around the country, it is possible to have conferences online. Attendees just need to dial in and, as long as they have a good connection and a webcam, it is possible to have a conference without any travel.

Table 5 shows the advantages and disadvantages of video conferencing.

Advantages	Disadvantages
Much less expensive as there is no need to leave the office, so no hotel or travel costs. Communication is instant with no delay, which means there is no need to wait for a meeting to happen at a later date and delay a project. Faster than other forms of communication and it includes being able to see the other person. Can include additional information, such as slides or presentation notes which can be added as an attachment. Reduces the need to have so many face-to-face meetings. Can be used to help with training or support employees at different locations. Avoids the cost of employee time being spent in traffic jams or being delayed going to or from a meeting.	Requires equipment with internet access but, with increasingly powerful phones or laptops, this is becoming less of a disadvantage. Relies on a good internet connection so can be slow or more challenging if the Wi-Fi connection is weak. Not the same as face-to-face communication as it doesn't allow people to completely interact, e.g. shake hands. Security problems due to others hacking in and getting information that they should not have access to. The software may need to be purchased, which will cost the organisation money.

Table 5: The advantages and disadvantages of video conferencing

Internet and website development

The internet and websites are also constantly in development, and this means that your organisation needs to keep up to date with these technological changes, too.

Having a good website is important so that customers can book with your organisation or purchase items. If your website is not secure, your organisation could be hacked or face other security problems. This could compromise the personal data that your company holds, which has legal implications (see Chapter 4).

Other key problems associated with not developing your organisation's website include:

- the organisation looking outdated

- a fall in customer trust as it appears that the organisation does not care.

E-commerce

E-commerce is buying or selling services or goods online. Most organisations have websites. If they are kept up to date, there are many ways that a website can be used, including being linked to promotional offers through advertising or targeted emails.

E-commerce allows organisations to share information such as production schedules, delivery schedules and appointments. It is now so popular that for most organisations it is not possible to work effectively without an instant online process.

How much is mobile technology going to affect your role in the next year?

E-commerce also reduces the need for processing or printing information as customers can bring their mobile devices and use these to, for example, gain access to a venue for a pre-booked event. E-commerce also helps manage event numbers more carefully as events can be booked in advance and venues changed to accommodate more or fewer attendees.

E-commerce has changed the way that the administration role works. With online ordering, tracking of parcels by customers and even self-service access to change details, customers can do much more for themselves. This means that the administration role has changed to be more one of quality assurance and support than data entry.

Social networking

E-commerce often links to social networking. Although social networking sites started as social spaces, many organisations now use them to advertise, promote their organisations and gain valuable feedback from their customers.

Social networking can be used at short notice to make customers aware of an event or activity and how they can be involved. It can be used to reach new customers or make suppliers aware of what is happening in your organisation.

Your organisation may also use social networking to communicate with employees, particularly if you work for a large organisation with many office sites. Employees can be kept up to date with what is happening or about events.

However, there are some key risks involved with social media including:

- the reputation of the organisation may be viewed negatively depending on the information put out on social media

- care needs to be taken with issues such as 'fake news'

- customers or other stakeholders can use social media to give negative feedback which can be shared widely and is difficult to control.

Environmental factors

Environmental factors look after the environment and make sure that the organisation operates ethically, helping to reduce its impact on the environment.

Influence of ethical practices

Ethical practice is the way that an organisation conducts itself. It is not just about complying with UK environmental laws but can also have higher moral or **ethical standards**. There are five ways that all organisations can seek to behave more ethically.

Reducing carbon footprint

An organisation's 'carbon footprint' measures the impact that its activities have on the environment. The carbon footprint itself is measured in units of carbon dioxide, a gas that harms the environment. The ideal is to have a carbon footprint as small as possible by reducing the amount of energy that your organisation uses for heating, food and transport. Packaging goods is also part of the carbon footprint as energy is needed to make the packaging; this adds to the carbon footprint.

Environmental laws aim to help reduce our carbon footprint by making some negative practices illegal.

At work you can reduce your carbon footprint in many ways including:

* turning off lights and using energy-saving bulbs
* boiling only the water that is needed for cups of tea or coffee, rather than boiling the whole kettle
* lowering the temperature in the office by 1°C, which reduces energy use
* avoiding unnecessary travel or using video conferencing
* recycling plastic, avoiding plastic coffee cups and purchasing low-plastic items or those that are made from recycled sources, such as recycled printer paper.

Reducing waste

Reducing waste at work is another way of reducing the impact that your organisation has on the environment. Reducing the amount of waste that your organisation produces has three major benefits. First, there is less impact on the environment. Second, there is less need to process waste or have it sent to landfill. Finally there is a non-environmental benefit: reducing waste makes the organisation more efficient so the organisation will need to buy less of the material or supplies in the first place, meaning the organisation has more funds to spend elsewhere or more profit.

Common ways for organisations to reduce waste at work include:

* water fountains or reusable bottles/glasses for drinks rather than plastic bottles
* reducing unnecessary packaging or asking suppliers to avoid using plastic
* avoiding printing documents and using online versions instead

- replacing equipment only when essential or replacing it with recycled items
- giving used equipment to charities rather than sending it to landfill
- disposing of electrical items to ensure that parts are recycled into other products.

Using locally sourced materials or products

Buying from local producers has many benefits and is an example of ethical practice. Sometimes the cost may be higher for the initial purchase but the reduced cost to the environment and local benefit is huge as it can: reduce travel costs, develop links with local suppliers, help people to work locally and build sustainable communities.

Fair trade partnerships

'Fair trade' is organisations working together to help suppliers so that fair prices are paid for goods. This is particularly the case for goods that are produced by farmers in developing countries. By using fair trade partnerships, producers are paid a fair price for their products. Although this may cost more for your organisation, it is viewed as ethical and more sustainable.

Supply chains

Organisations also have to think about the environmental impact of their supply chain. This is important because being ethical at every stage means that the whole organisation is ethical. It can include fair trade purchasing. It can also involve avoiding organisations where there are concerns about poor ethical records, such as the use of child labour.

Rise and importance of sustainability

Environmental sustainability has a big environmental impact as it means resources are not being used that cannot be replaced, or materials are being used more than once. Table 6 shows the impact of environmental sustainability.

Key term	

Environmental sustainability – Making sure that organisations use resources that are renewable or recyclable.

Sustainable action	Impact on the organisation
Increasing pressure to use renewable energy sources	Organisations are increasingly being asked to use energy sources that are greener and cleaner. These sources include solar energy, where energy can be created from sunlight and either be used by the organisation or sold to energy suppliers. Wind or wave power, depending on where the organisation is located, are also possible.
Using recyclable materials	Recycling is key for organisations, whether that is purchasing goods that have already been recycled, e.g. paper, or whether the organisation has its waste recycled and then reused. Using recycled materials and reusing waste means the organisation is much more sustainable as raw materials are not reduced and can continue to be reused in the future.

Table 6: The impact of environmental sustainability

Market forces

Market forces are the change in the number of people or organisations that want goods or services. This desire leads to greater or shorter **supply** (or availability of those goods). When there is too much **demand**, generally this leads to prices going up because the goods or services are rarer. When demand is low, prices generally go down.

Increase or decrease in demand for goods or services

In your workplace, you will be aware when you are busier as you have more clients or customers demanding goods or services, and times when you are quieter. This is being aware of the market forces at work. Table 7 sums it up.

Demand	Impact on goods and services
Increases	More people want to purchase goods or services, so this may affect availability of appointments or the length of time that it takes to offer goods or services.
	Having a big increase in demand can affect the reputation of your organisation if customers are disappointed and unable to buy what they want, when they want it.
Decreases	Fewer people want to purchase goods or services. This means there will be less income coming into the organisation from orders and if you sell goods they will need to be stored.
	When demand decreases, organisations often have a promotion or sale to increase demand.

Table 7: The impact of changing demand

Increases or decreases in demand can happen for lots of different reasons including changes in the seasons, fashion changes or celebrity endorsements.

Increase or decrease in costs of goods and services

If there is an increase in the number of people who want particular goods or services, this usually means that the price of those goods or services increases. This is because 'market forces' – the power of the people who are seeking to buy those goods or services – drive up prices. Businesses who know that their goods or services are heavily in demand can charge more and it is likely that customers will be willing to pay.

If there is a decrease in demand for goods and services, the opposite happens. With too many goods on offer, the organisation may need to reduce prices by having a sale or a promotion to encourage sales.

Organisations are also affected by market forces that change the cost of goods or services that they buy. These may be direct costs or indirect costs.

- If the raw materials used to make a product increase in price, this is a direct cost. If this was your organisation, it would need to raise prices to cover its costs.

- If there are other cost increases across the UK that also affect your organisation, such as an increase in tax on fuel, this will be an indirect cost that will make your goods or services more expensive.

Your organisation may be more or less affected by increasing or decreasing costs depending on whether what you offer is an essential or a luxury item.

Availability of goods or services

You have learned about demand for products being affected by sudden changes in fashion choices or celebrity endorsements, but availability of goods also affects the demand for goods.

Reasons why goods or services are not available can vary. For example, the impact of war or a natural disaster in a country where goods are produced, or where raw materials are sourced, can reduce availability significantly. Other factors that affect the purchase of goods or services include:

- the number of producers of goods in a market – if there are lots of manufacturers producing similar goods, then your organisation has more choice about who to buy from so goods are more likely to be available

- unexpected changes in the weather which may affect availability of goods as many producers predict demand based on the conditions of the previous year – if the weather is hotter than expected, the demand for related goods goes up and vice versa if the weather is cooler than predicted

- an inability to transport the goods to a particular country or area because of transport or import issues

- a lack of skills in your area which may affect your organisation's ability to offer a good or service if there are too few people who are trained in a particular skill.

Legal factors

Legal factors affect the way that your organisation operates. Legal factors include regulations and laws that cover data protection, health and safety, equality and other areas impacting your organisation.

Introduction of new legislation

New laws affect both the way that you work as an employee and your organisation as a whole. It is vital that your organisation keeps up to date with new legislation as 'We didn't know' is not a legal defence if you do something wrong. The type of law that will affect your organisation depends on the nature of its work and the sector it operates in.

New laws are put forward to parliament as bills that are read in the House of Commons. They are then passed on to the House of Lords and receive Royal Assent from the Queen before becoming law. Laws in force that may have affected your organisation include:

- apprenticeship levy tax – which requires medium and larger employers to pay tax that can be spent on training apprentices

- consumer protection laws – that give customers greater rights

- legislation about product packaging – such as the selling and packaging of tobacco products which was significantly changed in 2017 and affected retailers and manufacturers

- environmental issues – such as microbeads, which were banned from manufacturing under the Environmental Protection (Microbeads) (England) Regulations 2017

- the Automated and Electric Vehicles Act – this brought in measures relating to driverless cars and guidance for public charging of electric vehicles.

The government continues to put new legislation in place. For example, in 2018 the government, through its clean air policy, decided that certain wood burning stoves would be banned by 2022 due to the negative impact they have on the environment and air quality. Any organisation selling such stoves – or the wood that is used to fuel them – is affected by this change, impacting on the way it conducts its business.

All organisations need to make sure they consider guidance and changes in legislation and take part in consultations that may affect the way that they work.

Changes to existing legislation

Updates and changes to existing laws and regulations also affect the way that your organisation operates. You learned about this in Chapter 4 with the impact of GDPR on existing data protection law. It is important for you and your employer to ensure that you are aware of any changes in law that affect your organisation.

Go to www.legislation.gov.uk and view the legislation that is currently being passed. Consider the possible impact of it on your organisation and your role.

Summary

In this section you have learned about external factors. It has covered:
- understanding relevance of external factors to your organisation
- understanding the international/global market in which your organisation is placed.

Activities

▶ Activity 1: UK Foreign and Commonwealth Office

Find out more about international relations between the UK and other countries by accessing the Foreign and Commonwealth Office website. Review which countries have been visiting the UK, which countries the UK is working with, and the latest speeches and statements by the UK government's ministers.

▶ Activity 2: Bank of England base rate

Carry out research to find out the current Bank of England base rate. Compare it with 12 months ago, 3 years ago and 5 years ago.

How has it changed?

What impact has this had on you and your organisation?

▶ Activity 3: VAT rates

Go to www.gov.uk/vat-rates and find out the current rate of VAT and which goods or services are exempt.

How does this affect the products or services that your organisation offers?

▶ Activity 4: Skills at your organisation

Consider how your organisation is directly or indirectly affected by skills shortages.

Ask your line manager about the skills that your organisation is finding it hard to find. What are they doing to reduce the impact of these skills shortages?

Is there any training that is offered to existing staff that can be used to try to reduce the impact?

How does this affect the salaries of staff who have skills that are highly in demand?

▶ Activity 5: Taxes

Write a list of all the different ways that your organisation pays tax and then find out the rates which are paid for these different types of tax.

Ask your line manager or the accountant at your workplace how the organisation is affected by tax.

▶ Activity 6: Government spending

Consider how your organisation is directly or indirectly affected by government spending.

You may have also heard of terms such as Brexit or austerity.

Carry out research into how these terms affect a fall or rise in different areas of government spending.

▶ Activity 7: Demographic profile

Produce a table for your portfolio that lists each of the five demographic influences and define their meaning.

Are people in your local community for each demographic area increasing or decreasing in number?

How does this affect your organisation and your role?

▶ Activity 8: Video conferencing

At work, you may already use video conferencing. If you do, answer the following questions and write a report for your manager.

- What are the advantages of using video conferencing?
- Are there any disadvantages?
- How does this type of conferencing affect minute-taking and other administrative matters?

If you don't use video conferencing, produce a short report for your line manager on the advantages and disadvantages of using it at your organisation.

▶ Activity 9: Local community

Think about the area(s) where your organisation operates and the trends that have been happening.

How has the media affected perceptions of your organisation and what it does?

How has it been affected by crime directly or indirectly (for example through insurance premium changes)?

What impact has education had on your area and the number of people with different types of qualifications?

How have working patterns changed?

Have a discussion with your line manager or another member of staff who has worked at the organisation for several years and ask them how they think changes in society's behaviour have affected your organisation.

▶ Activity 10: Technology

Review the questions and produce responses for each. Where you don't know the answer, discuss it with your line manager.

- How much is mobile technology going to affect my role in the next year?
- How will it be affected in the next three years?
- Which additional resources will we need?
- What additional training will I need to operate that equipment?

Topic consolidation

▶ Test yourself

1. Political factors
- ☐ I understand what is meant by government intervention.
- ☐ I can name the largest political parties in the UK.
- ☐ I can describe, with examples, what is meant by inflation.
- ☐ I can provide definitions, with examples, of monetary policy, fiscal policy and government spending.
- ☐ I need to review my understanding of government, monetary policy, fiscal policy and government spending.

2. Economic factors
- ☐ I am clear about the impact of the labour market on my role and organisation.
- ☐ I can describe the impact of skills shortages on my organisation.
- ☐ I understand how increasing or decreasing costs impact my organisation and what is meant by the supply chain.
- ☐ I need to find out more about how economic factors affect my role and my organisation.

3. Social factors
- ☐ I can describe different trends in society's behaviour.
- ☐ I can give judgements about how beliefs affect the way that people behave in the UK, and the impact on me and my organisation.
- ☐ I know what is meant by social responsibility and how it affects my role.
- ☐ I understand what is meant by demographics and how this affects my organisation.
- ☐ I am not clear about how social factors affect my organisation.

4. Technological factors
- ☐ I know how changes in technology are affecting my organisation and those in the supply chain.
- ☐ I am clear about the benefits and drawbacks of video conferencing on my organisation.
- ☐ I can make judgements about how the internet and website developments and/or e-commerce are having an impact on my role and organisation.
- ☐ I can make judgements about social networking in relation to my role but also make recommendations for the wider business community.
- ☐ I am not clear how technological factors are affecting my organisation and my role at work.

5. Environmental factors
- ☐ I can describe what is meant by a carbon footprint and how it relates to my own role and that of my organisation as a whole.
- ☐ I can describe four ways my organisation could help to reduce waste and the impact of buying local.
- ☐ I know what is meant by fair trade partnerships and the supply chain.
- ☐ I am unclear about the impact of environmental factors on my role and my organisation as a whole.

9

IT

IT

You need IT skills because most organisations rely on IT to operate efficiently. Some depend on IT totally while others may use just basic IT packages and systems. In all cases, the IT used has to be relevant to the organisation's needs if it is to operate successfully.

Sending emails

Emails are an integral part of most organisations' activities, so it is vital that any communication you carry out by email is professional and accurate. You also need to consider how you will organise and keep track of your emails.

Constructing a professional email

Subject line: This is your opportunity to attract the attention of the person you are emailing. Your subject line should communicate the purpose of your email and be brief. Always complete the subject line regardless of the length of your email.

Greeting: Always include a greeting. If you know the name of the person you are emailing, use it. You should call the person by their title (e.g. Mr, Mrs, Dr) unless you are on first-name terms with them.

Font style: Use a business-like font, avoiding any ornate or coloured fonts. Avoid writing in all capitals, and use lower-case letters like we do in this book.

Length: Keep your emails to the point and avoid unnecessarily long emails. Most people will skim-read long emails and vital information may be missed.

Layout: Break up the text in your email by using short sentences and paragraphs.

Emoticons: Avoid any emoticons such as smiley faces and other 'text speak' language when sending business emails.

Using cc and bcc: Before copying people in, be sure to think whether it is essential that they see the email. There may be occasions that you want to use blind copy (bcc), which will mean nobody else will see that that person has been copied in.

Sign off: End your email with an appropriate sign off. This can be as brief as 'thank you' or 'kind regards'. Most email software allows you to embed a signature – your name, job title/position and a business address – that you can use for all your emails.

Final checks: Read through the email to check that it is complete, makes sense and is accurate in its message. Check that any attachments you include are the right attachments and that you have copied the correct people into the email.

Spelling and grammar: Finally, always check for spelling, grammar and typing errors before pressing send. Remember that a spell checker may not pick up all of the errors.

Confidentiality: Once you have sent an email, its contents and any attachments are no longer in your control. Your email may be forwarded to others who will be able to scroll down and see all previous emails. You should always be mindful of what you say in a business email.

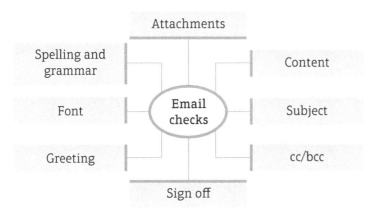

Figure 1: What checks do you make before sending an email?

Organising and keeping track of emails

Most email software packages allow you to organise your emails into folders. There are many ways you can categorise your folders: by person, by organisation, by priority and so on. It may be that your organisation has a policy of how emails should be organised or you may be able to create your own system.

You can read more about filing emails in Chapter 10.

How do you organise your emails? Can you improve your system?

Writing letters

Key terms

Template – A basic document that provides a framework that can be built on when writing a letter or other business communication.

Jargon – Words or expressions used by a profession or group that are difficult for others to understand.

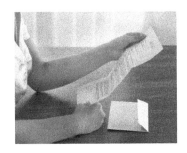

What letter templates are used within your organisation?

Behaviours

Professionalism – Behaves in a professional way. This includes: personal presentation, respect, respecting and encouraging diversity to cater for wider audiences, punctuality and attitude to colleagues, customers and key stakeholders.

There are several software packages you can use for writing letters. These packages usually allow an organisation to set up **templates**. You may be required to set up these templates, or they may be in place already.

Although emails are a quicker way of communicating than writing a letter, they may not get opened or may bypass the intended recipient, depending on the email address you have used. There will be times when it is more appropriate to send a letter by post, or you may be required to attach a letter to an email as an attachment.

The rules that you should follow when writing a letter are shown in Table 1.

Your address	Your organisation's address should always be on the letter. Any official stationery for your organisation is likely to already include the address and other contact details, such as telephone number, email address, website, etc. If the address is not included on the headed paper, you must make sure that you add it.
Recipient's address	You should also include the address of the person you are writing to, which is usually placed underneath your organisation's address.
Date	Always include the date on your letter. It can be placed on either the left- or right-hand side of the letter. You should write the month in full, for example '10 January 2019'.
Greeting	You should use the surname and title of the person you are writing to, if you know them. If you do not know their name, you should use 'Dear Madam' or 'Dear Sir'. If you know you are writing to a female and do not know if she uses 'Mrs' or 'Miss', you can use 'Ms'.
Body of letter	Write as simply and clearly as possible, avoiding **jargon** that the recipient is unlikely to understand. But do not use informal language, and don't use shortened words that you might find in text language.
Ending	'Yours faithfully' should be used when you do not know the name of the person you are writing to. 'Yours sincerely' should be used when you are using their name.
Your signature	You should sign your name and also type it underneath your signature.
Enclosures	If you are including any additional documents or paperwork with your letter, indicate this after your printed name by typing 'enclosures'. If you are sending a copy of the letter to anyone else, you should type 'cc' followed by their name or names, if there is more than one.

Table 1: Letter-writing rules

Creating proposals

When seeking approval to change a process or make an improvement to the organisation, you may be asked to put together a proposal.

Proposals are a way to pitch an idea to your organisation, along with any requirements needed for the project to be successful. A proposal should give a structured and logical argument for the improvements or changes you are suggesting and say how they will benefit your organisation.

There are several specialist software packages that can be used when creating a proposal or you may wish to create your own document. Whichever package that you choose should be able to pull together all the information you have in an exact and effective way. It should clearly explain the purpose of your project and meet any requirements unique to your proposal. If you are using your own document, you should ensure that each stage of your proposal is clearly shown.

Some proposal packages are **cloud-based** so they can be shared across a company or within a team. Others require installation onto your computer. There are also some that can be used via smartphones. When choosing which package, you need to consider:

- **collaboration** – this is where the software allows the users of the program to work together on the project

- **content repository** – this is a central place where information and completed documents can be stored and retrieved as required

- **document management** – documents need to be managed so that they can be updated, amended and changed as the project progresses, so it is a useful feature of any software program for project proposals

- **pipeline management** – this part of the software will manage the next stage or process of the project – having this feature in the software will help to ensure that each stage of the project proposal is fully completed, and nothing is missed

- **RFP (request for proposal) management** – having this feature within the software will help with the **procurement** and bidding process as the user will be able to create a brief that can be sent out as a request and/or invitation for interested parties to **tender** services that the organisation may be required to purchase to enable the project to move forward

- **templates** – help in the overall management – there may be some templates that are more useful than others and it is the role of the project manager to decide on the best templates to use.

There are comparison sites online that you can use to help you decide which proposal software might be best to use for your own project proposal.

Performing financial processes

There are several financial processes (covered in Chapter 6) that you will need to consider when creating a proposal. Using IT software such as spreadsheets or bespoke IT packages will help you accurately track all costs and income.

Spreadsheets

Spreadsheets can be used to help perform financial processes. The most widely used across most organisations is Microsoft® Excel®, which is part of its Office suite of IT software. Apple has its own version of spreadsheet software, called Numbers, and other manufacturers also have spreadsheets on the market.

There are several functions available within spreadsheets that can be used for financial processes and management, including calculations, reporting, creating graphs and tables, filtering/merging information, etc.

Other software packages

Aside from spreadsheets, there are several financial software packages available on the market. It will depend on the size of your organisation as to whether it is financially viable to invest in a financial software package or whether those you already have within your organisation are enough. If deciding to invest in a financial software package, you should consider the different features they may offer. Comparison websites can help you decide.

The benefits and drawbacks of using spreadsheets and bespoke financial software are shown in Table 2.

Spreadsheets		Bespoke financial packages	
Benefits	**Limitations**	**Benefits**	**Limitations**
Work well with small projects. Microsoft Office highly likely to already be installed within the organisation. Formulas can be used to ensure accurate figures are calculated.	Staff may not be able to use spreadsheets to their full potential. Costs in staff training so that spreadsheet use can be maximised. Data will only be as accurate as the input.	Software can be chosen to meet specific needs of the proposal. Many cloud-based versions, meaning several users can have access. Tracking finances can continue beyond an initial project proposal.	Likely to be expensive. Staff may not know all the features available within the software package. Time for training is likely to be required.

Table 2: Using IT for performing financial processes

'What if' scenarios

This will allow you to think about different approaches and possible ways to resolve issues. It may be that you have several different options; this feature would be useful to put each option into the software so that you can see the likely results and compare each.

Balance sheet

This function will enable you to ensure that the figures that you calculate for costs, expenses and so on will balance against income. Where the figures do not balance, you will be able to see the amount you are over or under to allow you to adjust your proposal.

Cash management

Depending on the size of your organisation, there may be large and small purchases to make. For your organisation to run smoothly, you will need to consider when you are likely to require cash, whether as actual cash or as a figure available to you, and where this money will come from. For example, is there an amount of cash put aside in an account ready for you to use, or will funds be made available at stages throughout a project? Will these funds rely on an income coming into the business or is it already available?

Forecasting

Forecasting is a tool that will help you to know when you need to purchase certain items and when the finance will be available. Forecasting will also allow you to consider anything that varies from what you were predicting and periods of time that you will need to be aware of, such as periods when an expenditure has been made but income may be delayed.

While forecasting can be done manually using a spreadsheet, having this feature as part of a software package is likely to be more accurate and it will be easier to make changes to the forecasting when needed.

General ledger

A general ledger records and tracks all financial activity. This feature will benefit your organisation as you will be able to create graphs and/or tables to demonstrate income and expenditure.

Income statements

This will be a useful feature if your organisation relies on income as funding. The income source can be identified and entered into the income statement software, stating how much is expected and by what means, e.g. through an allocated budget, a grant or income from sales.

Profit/loss statement

A project may not reduce costs or make money immediately; it may take time to see the benefits a project will bring. Using several profit and loss statements, you can show a timeline of the likely return on investment and when the benefits might be seen.

Choosing appropriate IT solutions

It is important that you can choose the most appropriate IT solution to resolve the problem you are facing within your organisation.

There are many IT solutions available. Some might already be installed within your organisation or you may be given an opportunity to research and buy additional IT solutions. You should consider what it is you need the software to do, the business needs and the skill levels of both yourself and others you work with.

If you are purchasing new IT solutions, it is important that you have a budget and that you stick to it. The more specialised the IT solution, the more expensive it is likely to be, and if you require a bespoke system there will be a premium to pay. The broader the requirements, the cheaper the software is likely to be.

Recording and analysing data

Using IT software will help you to organise your financial information so that managers can clearly see all costs and how the money and resources will be made available to meet the costs. The data you are required to record and analyse can be obtained from either the spreadsheet you have created to manage your financial processes or from any bespoke financial package your organisation may have.

Microsoft® Office or equivalent packages

Microsoft® Office is one of the most common software packages in organisations, so you should ensure that you are familiar with how to use it or equivalent packages.

Cloud-based applications

Cloud-based applications are increasingly popular as they offer a number of benefits, such as remote access and real-time updates as data is put into the system. Software upgrades from the company that produced the IT package may be implemented automatically and free of charge, so an organisation is always working with the latest version of the software – provided it has been bought on a licensing system.

Updating and reviewing databases

The data and information within a database will vary according to the type of organisation and the sector in which it operates. Organisations gather data for different purposes. For example, an optician will hold the medical history of patients, whereas a retailer will hold data on buying habits. In each case, the data is based on customer details and will need to be updated as the customer's information changes. The databases will need to be reviewed to ensure that information is still relevant and current.

Other databases may be based on your organisation's equipment or resources. These could include HR records on employees. These databases also need to be updated and reviewed to ensure that the data on them remains relevant and current. This helps ensure that it is a workable set of data that will give accurate information when required and analysed.

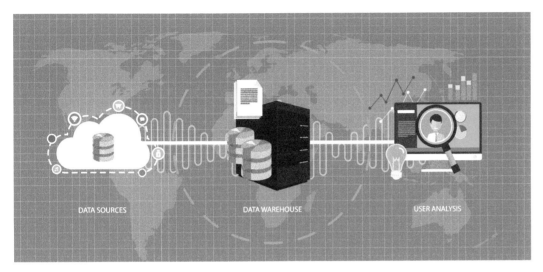

DATA SOURCES   DATA WAREHOUSE   USER ANALYSIS

What information does your organisation store on a database?

Recording information and producing data analysis

A business record is a document that records business activity, such as minutes of meetings, memos, employment contracts, accounting documents, budgets, customer and employee records, or equipment and resources records.

Some of these records will be analysed by an organisation to establish trends or gather intelligence on business activity. For example, an organisation may analyse data relating to employee records to establish the percentage of the workforce being promoted. This would be useful information for the company's planning or to establish additional staffing requirements while the organisation is going through an expansion programme.

In another example, an organisation may wish to establish the spending habits of their customers, which can be done through analysis of their customer database. Once an organisation can identify customer preferences, they can focus on maximising opportunities through targeted marketing campaigns.

Summary

In this section you have learned about the different aspects of IT that are required in your business administrator role. You have learned about using IT to communicate, create proposals and perform financial processes, as well as recording information and producing data analysis. This section covered how to use IT to support your organisation's activities such as:

- writing and sending emails and letters
- creating proposals using dedicated IT software
- performing financial processes
- using databases, recording and analysing the data.

Activities

▶ Activity 1: Creating and sending emails

Gather several business emails that you have recently sent. Go over each one and compare it against the checklist below. Make notes as to how your emails could be improved.

- Subject line completed?
- Correct greeting used?
- Appropriate font used?
- The right length?
- Correct layout?
- Correct spelling and grammar?
- Cc or bcc used?
- Sign off used?

What software package did you use when sending these emails?

What coaching have you given others in sending emails? What have you learned from this section of the book that you could use to coach others?

▶ Activity 2: Writing and sending letters

Gather several letters that you have created recently and sent, either as email attachments or that you have posted. Go over each of the letters and compare them against the checklist below. Make notes as to how they could be improved.

- Did you include your address?
- Did you include the recipient's address?
- Did you include the date and was it in the correct place on the letter?
- Did you use an appropriate greeting?
- Body of the letter: did you write inappropriately? Would you make any changes now you are re-reading it?
- Have you used an appropriate salutation?
- Did you include any enclosures and/or copy anyone in? If so, did you use the correct indicators?

Keep a diary of how you have coached others in writing and sending letters.

▶ Activity 3: Creating proposals

Gather information that you have researched for a project and complete an outline of your proposal.

From this outline, write a heading for each topic that you wish to cover and complete bullet-point notes under each that you can build upon.

Identify any areas where you have gaps or that need further research and development.

▶ Activity 4: Performing financial processes

Identify and list five financial processes that are part of your business administration role. Undertake research to establish the most appropriate IT software packages to use for each of the financial processes you have identified.

List the benefits and limitations of those you consider most appropriate.

Identify the people who will use and implement these processes and keep a diary of how you have coached others in using the software.

▶ Activity 5: Databases

Identify the databases that your organisation uses and find out the following.

- Which software package is used?
- What information is held in your organisation's database?
- Who is responsible for updating and reviewing the database?
- What is the process for updating the database?
- How often is the database reviewed?

What is your role in each point above/how can you become involved if you are not already?

▶ Activity 6: Recording information and producing data analysis

Identify the information that you record in your organisation and which information requires you to produce a data analysis. Answer the following.

- What information do you record and how?
- Of this information, which requires you to produce a data analysis?
- What analysis are you required to undertake for each?
- How do you present the data analysis?
- Who are you producing the data analysis for?

Collect evidence of recording information and producing data analysis.

▶ Activity 7: Definitions

Use the knowledge you have gained to write down the definitions for each of the following terms:

- Balance sheet
- Cash management
- Forecasting
- General ledger
- Income statement
- Profit/loss statement
- Cloud-based applications
- Database
- Data analysis
- Procurement
- Tender

Topic consolidation

▶ Test yourself

1. When sending an email, it is important that the font style is:
   - ☐ ornate.
   - ☐ colourful.
   - ☐ lower case.
   - ☐ font size 16.

2. When sending emails, it is important to:
   - ☐ check spelling and grammar.
   - ☐ check the time the email is sent.
   - ☐ limit the number of recipients.
   - ☐ use appropriate emoticons.

3. When typing in the date on a letter, it must be:
   - ☐ on the left.
   - ☐ on the right.
   - ☐ either left or right.
   - ☐ at the bottom.

4. When sending a copy of a letter to a third or more person, the following should be added:
   - ☐ bcc.
   - ☐ bc.
   - ☐ ccc.
   - ☐ cc.

5. RFP stands for:
   - ☐ require, follow up and present.
   - ☐ request for proposal.
   - ☐ request for perfection.
   - ☐ reference first product.

6. Pipeline management is:
   - ☐ managing and documenting each stage of a project proposal.
   - ☐ managing and documenting the finances of a project proposal.
   - ☐ managing and documenting all staff involved in a project proposal.
   - ☐ managing and documenting milestone dates in a project proposal.

7. A benefit of using spreadsheets is:
   - ☐ relatively low cost to the organisation.
   - ☐ everyone knows how to use a spreadsheet.
   - ☐ all businesses have Excel installed.
   - ☐ it is likely to be costly.

8. Benefits of bespoke financial packages can include:
   - ☐ relatively small costs to the organisation.
   - ☐ that training is likely to be required.
   - ☐ that there may be hidden functions that staff are unaware of.
   - ☐ that the software can be cloud-based.

10

Record and document production

Record and document production

Records and business documents include business activities such as meeting minutes, memos, contracts, accounting documents, budgets, customer and employee records, equipment and resources records, and so on. They must be produced accurately if your organisation is to really know what is going on within it, so this is a very important part of your business administrator role.

Handling emails, letters and files

You learned in Chapter 9 how to use IT to produce emails and letters, among other documents. But handling them requires a slightly different set of skills.

Emails

Emails are likely to be stored electronically in virtual folders within an organisation's shared drives. It is possible to use email software, such as Microsoft® Outlook® and Apple® Mail software, to create folders that you can use to organise and store important emails.

Organising emails

Most email software has the functionality to create email folders. These categories might include a 'To do' folder or an archive; you may wish to organise your folders by project titles or by the name of the sender(s). Whichever system you choose to file and store the emails that you wish to keep, it is important that they are easily retrievable, and that you only save emails that are important.

Creating mailing lists

This is a useful function if you regularly need to send an email to the same group of people. Email packages allow you to create a mailing list which includes the email addresses of a number of people. Rather than typing each address each time, you can just select to send to everyone on the mailing list. This will save you time and ensure that you do not forget to include someone.

You must remember to update the mailing lists regularly and be aware of data protection regulations (see Chapter 4) and sharing email addresses within the whole group.

Sharing documents

Sending documents as attachments is an efficient way of sharing them with colleagues. Your organisation may have a storage limit on individual email accounts; this may mean some documents are too large to send. As an alternative, you should be aware of cloud-based file-transfer solutions such as WeTransfer that you can use to send large files.

Discussing business decisions

Because email is used as the main communication channel in many organisations, it can result in a long trail of emails sent between many people. While this is a useful record of who has said what, it can also lead to confusion and misunderstandings.

When using email for business conversations and decision making, ensure that your emails are to the point and that the language is appropriate. Once you have sent an email, you have no control over who can view that information.

Legal documents

Emails are legal documents of record. For example, if you reply to an email that sent you a contract as an attachment by saying, 'That looks fine,' you could be held to the contract even if you have not read it thoroughly. You should treat email correspondence in the same way you would written correspondence when used for business purposes.

Letters

Letters are still used by many businesses. Although they are likely to be created electronically (see Chapter 9), they may be stored electronically or in a filing system. This will largely depend on whether the letter is sent as an attachment to an email or printed out and posted to the recipient.

Your organisation will have its own policies around delivering letters which you must familiarise yourself with.

Creating letters

In your role, you may need to write and create the letters that you send, or you may use templates for regular communication. See Chapter 9 for more information.

Filing and storing

Whether the system in your organisation is electronic or paper-based storage, it is important that any letters written or received by your organisation are accessible and retrievable. See the section on *Files* on the next page for more information.

Formal record

Letters create a formal record of communication. When an organisation requires confirmation that a letter has been received, you can use specific postal services such as recorded or signed-for delivery, where a signature is required from the receiver.

How does your organisation file the letters that it sends and receives?

Files

Files may be stored electronically or in a paper-based system. It is important that you are aware of the different filing systems that may be used within your organisation and that you can use them efficiently and accurately. They are outlined in Table 1.

Filing system	What is it?	Benefits	Limitations
Alphabetic	Files or records are kept in alphabetical order. Files can be arranged by individual or business name, by topic or by geographical location, etc.	Works well for smaller systems which may include individual customer or business records.	Is difficult to manage when records or items to be filed exceed 5,000.
Numeric	Files are numbered and then filed in sequential order.	Filing and retrieving records is quicker. Can give increased confidentiality when customer names are replaced by numbers. The capacity of a numerical filing system is infinite.	A system needs to be in place to ensure that it is possible to find out which number refers to which name.
Alphanumeric	Alphabetical and numeric systems combined. Typically, records are filed alphabetically and then categorised numerically within each letter.	It can increase the capacity of an alphabetic system.	Will only work well with a detailed index to assist in filing and retrieving records.
Paperless	A system of storing files electronically, which can be developed by creating folders within the organisation's shared drive or software program.	Minimises the risk of misplaced files, allowing for efficient filing, storage and retrieval of records. Removes physical storage needs. Systems can be shared across an organisation and viewed remotely by authorised users.	Systems that over time grow on an organisation's shared drive may lead to duplication and 'lost' files.

Table 1: Different filing systems

Payments

It is essential that any payments made by your organisation are accurate and are made on time. There are many accountancy packages and software programs available to help a business make quick and easy payments.

Any payments made by your organisation will often be triggered by an invoice sent by your suppliers. These will include the date by when the invoice must be paid. Other payments are likely to be for small items and may be taken from petty cash.

BACS

BACS payments are payments made by online banking. (BACS stood for Bankers' Automated Clearing Services, although it's now run by a company called BACS Payment Schemes Limited.)

To make a BACS payment, you need the sort code, account number and a reference so that your supplier can link your organisation's payment to a specific invoice. Once the supplier has been set up as a payee, payments can be set up as a standing order for regular payments or manually triggered for individual payments.

Accuracy is essential as your organisation will be responsible for any incorrect data entered. Incorrect information could result in the money going to an incorrect payee.

It will probably depend on the size of your organisation as to who manages BACS payments. Large organisations will have an accounts department, whereas in a smaller organisation you may be required to make payments yourself.

If your organisation has an accounts department, you may be required to authorise any payments that are scheduled to be made by confirming that the payment due is correct and that the goods or services have been received.

Credit cards

You may be able to use a business credit card to pay suppliers. Charges may be added if you use a business credit card, particularly if any outstanding amounts are not settled each month.

Paying by credit card will give your organisation additional credit facilities and is a useful method of payment if funds are not available right away but spending is required by your organisation immediately.

Cash

Cash is now rarely used in business and is likely to be limited to small purchases such as stamps or office refreshments where cash is taken from a float, known as petty cash.

Smaller organisations are most likely to use a petty cash system. Larger organisations may have a 'no cash' policy; items such as postage are provided through a designated post room and a staff canteen is available for refreshments.

Reports and proposals

When writing a report or proposal (see Chapter 9), it is essential that the content is relevant and meets the requirements of your organisation. Your report or proposal will be read by others. You must consider the format and ensure that the message is clear.

There are eight key steps that will help you write a meaningful and useful report or proposal. These steps are shown in Table 2.

How do you use reports to influence others in your organisation?

Step	Report and proposal writing
1. Know your purpose	What is the reason for writing your report? Is it to inform, explain and/or persuade? Defining your main aim will give you focus and should drive everything else in your report.
2. Know your readers	Who is your audience? What do they already know? What is their attitude? What pre-conceived ideas might they have? Will they need persuading?
3. Know your objective	What do you want your reader to do after reading your report? How can you match the purpose to the reader? Once you have answered those two questions, you will be able to write your objective. When the purpose of your report is to make changes, you should produce a logical and researched argument.
4. Choose an approach	Starting with a brief explanatory paragraph defining your research will put your report into context. This is known as an abstract or 'terms of reference'. You will also need to establish the information you need and how much of it to complete your report. Then you can decide how you will present the information within it, for example using paragraphs or bullet points.
5. Decide on a structure	Depending on the importance of your report, it should contain some or all the following: • a title page • an index • an abstract or terms of reference • an introduction (sometimes called an executive summary) • background to the issue • the procedure • implications (or issues) • solutions (or recommendations) • a conclusion • appendices • a bibliography (or references).
6. Use the right style	The style of your report should reflect its importance and the audience you are addressing. Reports should be simple, clear and easy to read and any statements should be backed up with facts, figures and/or a justification.
7. Consider the layout	Use an appropriate style, size and colour of font. Only use visuals where they will add value to the report. This may be in the form of graphs, charts or pictures. Use explanatory captions below any visuals to connect them to the report content.
8. Leave time to refine	Give yourself enough time to review your report and make any adjustments. If there is time, ask a trusted person to read through the report and give feedback.

Table 2: Steps for producing a report or proposal

Suggesting improvements and respecting confidentiality

It is important that you handle your organisation's records and documents in a way that respects confidential information. You may spot ways that your organisation's record-handling processes can be improved.

Suggesting improvements and presenting solutions to management

When making recommendations for improvements to the way that your organisation produces and handles records and documents, you could use a report or proposal that you have written to back up your ideas and suggestions. You should clearly set out the improvement opportunities you have identified and why you are recommending them.

Your recommendations may be for minor improvements or for larger, significant improvements where you need to demonstrate your leadership skills by involving others and providing direction.

You can read more about suggesting improvements to processes in Chapter 7.

Handling confidential information

When handling personal data it is vital that you follow your organisation's procedures and policies. These will have been designed to meet legislative requirements such as the Data Protection Act 2018 and GDPR (the General Data Protection Regulation). These give people such as your organisation's clients or customers certain rights to privacy and confidentiality.

Failure to follow the procedures and policies designed by your organisation could result in an investigation by the Information Commissioner's Office (ICO), which is an independent body established to uphold information rights.

To comply with GDPR regulations, an organisation must:

- ask for consent from those whose data they hold – this must be a clear process where the individual must 'opt in'. An organisation cannot use pre-ticked boxes and must make it clear to individuals:
  - the name of the organisation
  - the name of any third-party controllers who will reply on the consent
  - why the organisation wants the data
  - what the organisation will do with the data
  - that individuals can withdraw their consent at any time

- record that they have asked for consent from an individual by keeping a record of when and how they obtained the consent and keeping a record of exactly what the individual was told at the time

- manage the consent by updating records and having processes in place to refresh the consent, as well as making it easy for individuals to withdraw their consent.

See Chapter 4 for more about relevant legislation.

What are your organisation's procedures for handling confidential information?

Your role might involve supporting a disciplinary hearing involving another colleague. You should respect that colleague's right to privacy and avoid gossiping with other people about what you hear or read when it involves HR issues.

Even non-personal data can be confidential. For example, meetings that you attend or reports that you read may include information that your organisation does not want to get into the hands of its competitors. If the information 'leaked', it might give your organisation's competitors an advantage. You should think carefully before discussing your organisation's affairs with people from outside the organisation.

Coaching others to complete these tasks

There are several coaching models that you can use when coaching others in record and document production. Three models are shown in Table 3, Table 4 and Table 5. Each takes a slightly different approach. You should use the model – or a combination of models – that best suits your coaching style.

Goal	Guide your team member into identifying their goal. What is it that they wish to achieve? How will they know that their goal has been achieved? How does the goal fit in with the team member's personal development plan or career objectives?
Reality	Help your team member recognise their current reality rather than tell them. If they find this difficult, you can help them by asking questions such as, 'What is happening now?', 'Have you taken any steps towards your goal?', 'Does this goal conflict with anything else?'.
Options	Encourage your team member to explore all the options available to them. You can offer suggestions, but you should let your team member try to come up with their own first. Discuss with your team member to decide which options to progress.
Way forward	Your team member should think about the next steps. Once SMART objectives have been set (based on the goals established at the first stage) and options identified, a plan of action can be drawn up. Guide and support your team member in creating the action plan, but they should decide on the actions agreed and write up their own plan.

Table 3: How to use the GROW model

Contract	During the initial discussion with your team member, establish how the coaching will be undertaken. Agree the ground rules, ensuring that you are both open and honest, and help your team member to set their outcomes.
Listen	Actively listen to your team member so that you can gain an understanding of their situation.
Explore	Through discussion, help your team member to understand the impact their current situation may be having on them. You can then challenge your team member to think through possible resolutions.
Action	Guide your team member to decide how they are going to make progress. Encourage them to write an action plan with deadlines. It is good practice to keep a copy of the action plan for your own records.
Review	Review what you covered during the coaching meeting. Confirm what was discussed and ask your team member for feedback on how the coaching session helped them. Find out if there is anything they would like to do differently next time and what they liked about the session.

Table 4: How to use the CLEAR model

Frame the conversation	At the first stage of the coaching session, focus on what your team member wishes to achieve. Agree on the purpose of the coaching, the process that will be followed and what the outcomes will be.
Understand the current state	Guide your team member into understanding what their current situation is. Ask questions throughout the discussion so that you can see things from their perspective. Be consistent and impartial during the discussions.
Explore the desired state	The next step is to help your team member think about where they would like to be at the end of the coaching sessions – their desired state. You should help them through discussion to generate different and alternative paths to get to this desired state.
Lay out a plan for success	The final stage is to create an action plan with SMART outcomes. Ensure that your team member draws up an action plan that details the desired outcomes with the specific steps they will need to take in order to achieve it.

Table 5: How to use the FUEL model

Summary

In this section you have learned about producing and handling a variety of records and documents that you are likely to use in your role as a business administrator, as well as how you might use some of these to make recommendations for improvement. You learned about keeping these records confidential and how you might coach others in the processes to complete these tasks. This section has covered:

- producing, maintaining and drafting accurate records and documents that include emails, letters, files, payments, reports and proposals that comply with your organisation's confidentiality procedures
- making recommendations for improvements and presenting solutions to management
- coaching models including GROW, CLEAR and FUEL.

Behaviours B

Professionalism – Behaves in a professional way. This includes: personal presentation, respect, respecting and encouraging diversity to cater for wider audiences, punctuality and attitude to colleagues, customers and key stakeholders.

Responsibility – Demonstrates taking responsibility for team performance and quality of projects delivered. Takes a clear interest in seeing that projects are successfully completed and customer requests handled appropriately. Takes initiative to develop own and others' skills and behaviours.

Activities

▶ Activity 1: Drafting correspondence

Gather a variety of business letters that you have created that demonstrate how you have been consistently accurate.

Categorise the correspondence to identify any letters where you used a template and letters that you drafted independently.

Choose the best of this evidence to put into your portfolio to showcase your skills in drafting correspondence that is consistently accurate.

Add notes to each piece of evidence to demonstrate how you have consistently ensured you have met requirements for confidentiality and followed the correct processes of your organisation.

▶ Activity 2: Writing reports

Undertake research within your organisation to identify any templates that should be used when writing a report.

Identify colleagues who have experience of writing reports and ask them if you can read through their reports to look for style and structure. Analyse how these reports were effective and successful. Ask your colleagues if there is anything they would do differently if they were to write the report again and why.

Using example reports, identify techniques and approaches that you could use in your own reports.

From your research, draft an outline of your approach to writing a report and the structure you would use.

▶ Activity 3: Reviewing others' work

List those whose work you regularly review. What mechanisms are in place for reviewing this work? How is the review recorded?

Practise using coaching models in order to support and give feedback to those whose work you review.

Gather evidence of reviewing others' work, showcasing good examples for your portfolio and to use during the portfolio interview.

▶ Activity 4: Maintaining records and files

Complete a table similar to the one below to identify the records and files that you maintain.

Gather evidence to confirm you have maintained these records and/or files. This could be screenshots for electronic records and files.

Identify evidence to put into your portfolio to showcase your ability and the skills you consistently use to produce and maintain accurate records. This should also demonstrate how you keep them confidential by following your organisation's procedures. Put this evidence into your portfolio and be prepared to talk about it in your portfolio interview.

Name of record/file	Purpose	Your role in maintaining it

▶ Activity 5: Writing reports and proposals

Identify a report or proposal that you have written, or have been involved in, and answer the following questions.

- What is the purpose of the proposal?
- Who are or were the readers?
- What are the objectives?
- What approach was chosen?
- What is the structure of the proposal?
- What is the style of the report?
- Has an appropriate layout been used? Give reasons for your answer.

▶ Activity 6: Suggesting improvements and presenting solutions

Using the report or proposal from Activity 5, identify any improvements and/or solutions to identified problems and produce a PowerPoint® presentation outlining the key points.

Present this to your manager and ask for their feedback on how you have performed and what improvements you could make.

▶ Activity 7: Coaching models

Using your experience and knowledge gained from completing Activity 3, identify which of the coaching models aligns with your own organisation's methods of coaching.

You should write about:

- the benefits of the coaching model
- the limitations of the coaching model
- how the coaching model aligns to your own organisation.

Topic consolidation

▶ Test yourself

1. Using emails to share documents can be used to:
   - ☐ keep a record of the documents.
   - ☐ seek feedback.
   - ☐ ensure confidentiality.
   - ☐ ensure the recipient receives it.

2. An alphanumeric filing system:
   - ☐ sorts files by letter.
   - ☐ sorts files by number.
   - ☐ sorts files by letter then number.
   - ☐ sorts files by number then letter.

3. Referring to payments, the C in BACS stands for:
   - ☐ clearing.
   - ☐ continuous.
   - ☐ cautious.
   - ☐ counter.

4. The structure of a proposal should include:
   - ☐ a purpose.
   - ☐ an objective.
   - ☐ an agenda.
   - ☐ a title page.

5. GDPR stands for:
   - ☐ General Data Protection Rules.
   - ☐ General Data Protection Regulation.
   - ☐ General Data Processing Regulation.
   - ☐ General Data Processing Rules.

6. In the GROW model of coaching, W stands for:
   - ☐ withdraw.
   - ☐ wait.
   - ☐ way forward.
   - ☐ want.

7. The first stage of the FUEL model of coaching is to:
   - ☐ fuel the conversation.
   - ☐ frame the conversation.
   - ☐ follow the conversation.
   - ☐ find the conversation.

11

Decision making

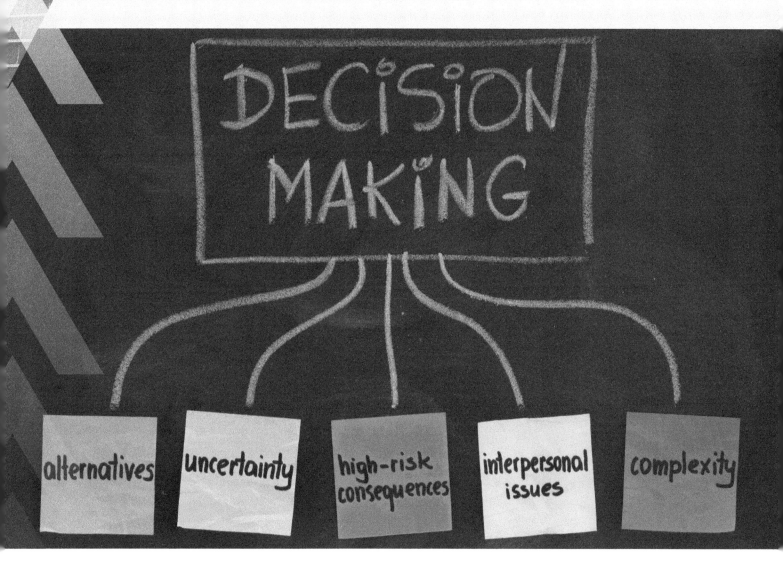

Decision making

Decision making is an important skill for you to develop. You will need to make decisions about how you carry out the tasks you are allocated – to make decisions about what you will do, how you will do it and when you need to complete it. Improving your decision-making skills and techniques will help you make well-informed decisions. You need to learn:

• how to use information from others to inform your decision making

• the steps used to make effective decisions

• how to deal with challenges in a mature way.

Problem-solving techniques

Key terms

Brainstorming – Developing and analysing creative ideas.

Workshop – A meeting to have an intensive discussion and analysis of a project or idea.

Behaviours

Managing performance – Takes responsibility for their own work, accepts feedback in a positive way, uses initiative and shows resilience. Also takes responsibility for their own development, knows when to ask questions to complete a task and informs their line manager when a task is complete. Performs thorough self-assessments of their work and complies with the organisation's procedures.

Adaptability – Is able to accept and deal with changing priorities related to both their own work and to the organisation.

In your role you will be faced with different problems that need to be solved effectively and efficiently. There are a number of different techniques you can use to help you solve problems and show good judgement. How to apply these techniques is covered in the next section, *Decision-making steps.*

Brainstorming

Brainstorming involves developing ideas either on your own or by working with others in your organisation. Everyone involved is encouraged to contribute as many ideas as they can regardless of how extreme or overly ambitious they may seem. The ideas are then discussed by everyone, analysing the pros and cons of each one and evaluating which ideas are the best.

Workshops

A **workshop** is a meeting with one item on the agenda: it focuses on an intense discussion about a project or idea. A workshop can be useful if you need to make decisions about what you and your team are going to do. You can get everyone who is involved together in one room and discuss all aspects of the project or idea, agreeing exactly what is going to be done and by who. You can also discuss and solve any problems you come across immediately, which may make the process faster and more effective.

SWOT analysis

A SWOT analysis allows you to consider the strengths and weaknesses of a project or idea, alongside the opportunities and threats that may affect it. Once you have done this you can start to decide whether the project or idea is worthwhile and what you should do to avoid the identified weaknesses and threats to make it successful.

You can read more about SWOT analysis in Chapter 16.

Use a SWOT analysis on one of your projects.

PESTLE analysis

PESTLE analysis is a decision-making tool that helps you analyse the effect on the project or idea of factors outside the organisation. It focuses on six groups of factors. Table 1 shows the six groups and gives examples.

Political	Economic
These are policies or initiatives that the government introduces or actions they take that may affect your project or idea. Examples: taxation levels, policies towards business.	These are factors related to the economy of the country. Examples: rate of **inflation**, standard of living, consumer spending, **economic growth**.
Social	**Technological**
These are factors related to society or the population of the country. Examples: trends and fashions, **demographics** and changes in lifestyle.	These are factors that involve changes or improvements in technology. Examples: new production processes, new products, innovation in markets, improvements in mobile technology.
Legal	**Ethical/environmental**
These factors relate to laws and legislation put in place by the government. Examples: health and safety laws, the minimum wage, employment law.	These are factors that affect the environment. Examples: pollution or impact on the carbon footprint. It also includes ethical issues. Examples: buying from suppliers that treat their workers fairly.

Table 1: Factors considered in a PESTLE analysis

Risk analysis

Risk analysis is a tool to identify all the things that can go wrong with a project or idea. Ask two questions:

- First, how likely is it that this will happen?

- Second, what can you do to avoid it?

Based on your answers, you can decide whether it is worth undertaking the project or idea and what you need to do to avoid the risks and make sure it is successful.

Key terms

PESTLE analysis – An analytical tool used to consider all the external factors that affect an organisation, project or idea.

Inflation – The general rise in average prices in a country.

Economic growth – An increase in the value of goods and services produced by the country.

Demographics – The breakdown of a country's population into different characteristic groups, such as by gender, age or income.

Decision-making steps

When making decisions, it is important to take a systematic approach. Taking
the process step by step and considering every aspect at each stage will help
you make a well-reasoned decision. Figure 1 shows how to break down the
decision-making process into steps.

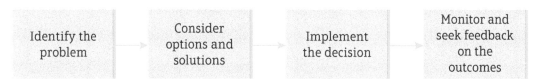

Figure 1: Break down the decision into key parts to help you

1. Identify the problem

Undertake problem analysis across all aspects of the problem to identify the
problem's causes and effects. This will help you start to think about a solution.

2. Consider options and solutions

Once you have identified all aspects of the problem, you can move on to the second
stage of the process, where you consider all the options and solutions.

Identify advantages and disadvantages of each possible solution

It is important that you identify the advantages and disadvantages of each possible
option so you can compare them with each other and help you decide which option
is best.

Identify potential problems and risks

Consider how likely it is that any potential problems and risks will occur and how
serious their impact would be on the organisation. This will help you plan to avoid
them but also help you choose the best solution.

Perform analysis

Analytical tools that will help you examine the options and solutions can be used at
this stage.

Adopt the recommendation

Once you have considered all the options, make a recommendation to the
organisation or others in the team, outlining the solution or option you think is best
and why. You may need to convince others that your recommendation is the right
thing to do, so prepare arguments in advance.

Make the decision

Once you have adopted the recommendation, make the final decision based on all the information and discussions that have taken place.

Take responsibility for the decision

When you have made the decision, you need to take responsibility for it and do all you can to ensure that it is successful. As a business administrator, you should stand by the decisions you have made and not blame others if things go wrong.

3. Implement the decision

You then need to implement the decision in the third stage of the process.

Act on the chosen solution

Put actions in place to carry out the decision. You should organise who will do what and when, checking progress to ensure that the solution is successful.

Set out standard operating procedures

Set and agree standard procedures for everyone to use when working to implement the decision. Share this with everyone so that your team is aware of how they should be working and to what standard.

Set SMART objectives

Ensure everyone on the team is aware of the overall objectives so they understand what they are working towards. Set yourself and anyone else involved their own individual SMART objectives, so they know what they need to do and by when.

Identify additional problems

As you implement the decision, further problems may arise that mean you need to make changes. It is important to identify these problems, ensuring that your team share any issues they face with you, so you can put strategies in place to correct them.

4. Monitor and seek feedback on the outcomes

The final stage of decision making involves monitoring the performance of the solution and seeking feedback on the outcomes.

Check success and achievement against objectives

Check how successful your solution has been, comparing it against the objectives you set so that you can judge its effectiveness. This demonstrates how well you have solved the problem and identifies areas for future improvement.

Gain feedback from users and other stakeholders involved in the process

Getting feedback from a range of different stakeholders who are involved in the process will help you to judge the level of success.

Record the outcomes

This might be in a report or document produced for your line manager or in a financial document. You may also want to record the outcomes of the solution to provide evidence for your end-point assessment or annual appraisal/performance review.

Sources of information

When making decisions, it is important to use a range of different sources of information to ensure that you have considered every possibility. This will help you avoid the risk of making a bad decision and acting in the wrong way. Here are some sources of information that you may be able to use to help you make decisions at work.

Customer feedback

Customers can be a vital source of information for informing your decisions. Customers are an important stakeholder for your organisation and you need to take their views seriously. Any feedback that they can offer, positive or negative, could be useful in helping you make decisions.

Monitoring data

As a business administrator, you will have access to a lot of your organisation's data. You can analyse this to help you make decisions and decide on actions you need to make to deal with issues.

Service level agreements (SLAs) and identifying service failures

Service level agreements (SLAs) are contracts between the service provider (the organisation or department that provides the service or product) and the end user (the customer or the other department of the organisation which uses the service or product). It agrees the level of service expected, including the standard of work, timescales and deadlines and any special agreements.

You should be aware of any SLAs in place in your organisation and the expectations that they create, and use them to help you make decisions about what you need to do and when.

Information from others in the organisation

You will also have the opportunity to gather feedback from your team and other people in your organisation to help inform your decision making. Though this is useful first-hand information from people you know, be aware that it may not always be the most accurate.

You can read more about seeking the views of experienced colleagues in the section on *Seeking advice from more experienced team members*.

Seeking advice from more experienced team members

Sometimes you will encounter issues that are very serious or that you are unsure how to deal with. You can seek advice from more experienced team members who can help you decide on what is the best thing to do.

It is better to ask for advice or to escalate the problem than to act badly and make the situation worse. You can talk to your line manager about when and how to escalate problems in the organisation.

Seeking guidance

Sometimes you may come across issues that you have not encountered before or do not know how to handle. In such situations, you could ask for advice or guidance about what you might do to solve the problem. This will help you maintain your authority and ensure that people in the organisation maintain their faith in you to make good decisions.

Communicating with more senior colleagues

You may also need to communicate with more senior colleagues. You will need to consider how you communicate with them to ensure that you maintain professionalism. You may work closely with some of these colleagues and therefore it might be appropriate to approach them informally to discuss the problem. However, you might have little involvement with others and you may need to follow formal and official procedures to escalate the issue.

Explaining the problem

Regardless of who you ask for advice, you will need to ensure you explain the problem clearly. You need to be calm, explaining exactly what has happened and what the problem is. If you have the opportunity, take time to collect your thoughts and write down a few notes so that you are clear about exactly what you need to say.

Follow escalation procedures

Every organisation will have escalation procedures in place. These are the processes and methods you use to bring problems and issues to the attention of higher levels of management within the organisation. The processes will outline what situations/ issues should be escalated and to who.

If you feel that after talking with more experienced colleagues you still cannot deal with the situation, you need to ensure that you follow the organisation's procedures to escalate the issue to someone more senior.

Acknowledging levels of authority

There will be an organisation structure in place, which outlines who is responsible for what and who has what authority. Be aware of the structure at your organisation so that you work within these levels of authority.

Dealing with challenges

As a business administrator, you will sometimes have to deal with challenges: from other members of staff, from suppliers or maybe from customers. This may be due to the pressure to complete tasks or because of mistakes made. It may be that a customer is making a complaint, or a supplier is unhappy with their treatment or lack of payment. All of these situations may result in you being challenged and having to hold difficult conversations.

The main thing when dealing with challenge is to act professionally and politely, helping you handle the challenge in a mature way. You need to consider the following.

- Think about the reasons for the challenge. Is it due to something that you have done or haven't done well? Is it that the person is frustrated and needs someone they can vent their emotions to? Is it that the organisation has let down its customers or suppliers?

- Listen carefully to what you are being told and calmly consider all the information provided. Asking questions may help you check the situation.

- At all times, be polite and professional. You will need to think carefully about the language you use and your tone of voice. You will also need to consider your body language to ensure that you do not come across as aggressive or confrontational.

- Be aware of your own emotions and those of others. You may feel out of your depth, frustrated or even angry. It is important for you to manage these emotions and remain calm and in control at all times. It is also important to show that you understand other people's feelings and demonstrate empathy to make them feel that you are taking their feelings and concerns seriously.

- Once you have decided on the reasons for the challenge, you need to consider how you are going to deal with the situation. Think about what you can do to resolve the situation and the actions that it requires. You may need to put an action plan together to help you resolve the issue.

You may find that you cannot resolve the challenging situation yourself and need to refer it to someone else in the organisation or ask for advice from a more experienced member of staff. You may need to get someone else involved who can mediate between you and the other people involved to help come to an agreed solution.

Summary

In this section you have learned about problem-solving techniques that can be used in the workplace. It has covered:
- types of information that can be used to help make decisions and guidance on how to use them effectively
- steps in the decision-making process and when to seek advice from others.

Activities

▶ **Activity 1: Problem-solving techniques (1)**

Think of a situation at work where you have had to:

- create new ideas
- decide how to carry out a task
- solve a problem.

How did you decide what to do? What technique or process did you use?

What techniques included in this chapter could you have used to help yourself?

▶ **Activity 2: Problem-solving techniques (2)**

Next time you have to make a decision, use one of the following techniques to help you make it:

- brainstorming
- risk analysis
- SWOT analysis
- PESTLE analysis.

Write a short report analysing how using the technique helped you make the decision.

▶ **Activity 3: Decision-making steps**

Think about a decision you need to make at work. Practise using the decision-making steps discussed in this section to help make the decision.

Make a note of the following to help you prepare for your professional discussion and competency-based interview:

- What did you do?
- What went well? What went badly?
- What decision did you make? Was it the correct one?
- What would you do differently next time?

▶ **Activity 4: Dealing with challenges**

Think of a situation where you have been challenged by someone at work. Consider the following.

- What did you do well?
- What did you do less well?
- What do you need to do to improve?
- What can you do to achieve this improvement?

▶ **Activity 5: Escalating challenges**

Investigate the structure and lines of authority in your organisation. Who could you escalate problems to? What procedure would you use to do this?

Topic consolidation

▶ Test yourself

1. When making decisions at work, do you:
   - ☐ find it difficult to decide?
   - ☐ decide immediately?
   - ☐ ask others for their opinions first?
   - ☐ leave it up to someone else to decide?

2. When using information you have gathered, do you:
   - ☐ accept the information is correct regardless?
   - ☐ triangulate the data with other sources?
   - ☐ ask others whether they think it looks right?
   - ☐ use information from lots of different stakeholders?

3. When handling problems at work, do you:
   - ☐ consult others about what they think you should do?
   - ☐ use problem-solving techniques to help you think through the problem?
   - ☐ consider all aspects of the problem, including its causes and effects?
   - ☐ think of a solution and action it as soon as you can?

4. If you need to escalate a problem to someone more senior, are you:
   - ☐ happy and relieved?
   - ☐ upset and disappointed?
   - ☐ uncomfortable and awkward?
   - ☐ disappointed but know it is the right thing to do?

5. When making decisions do you:
   - ☐ act quickly?
   - ☐ take time to consider options?
   - ☐ hold back and refer to your line manager?
   - ☐ use your initiative and ask questions?

6. When dealing with challenges, are you:
   - ☐ calm and in control?
   - ☐ stressed and anxious?
   - ☐ out of your comfort zone?
   - ☐ relaxed and detached?

7. If your decision is challenged, do you:
   - ☐ listen to others' points of view?
   - ☐ say you have made a mistake?
   - ☐ ignore what is being said?
   - ☐ refer to your line manager?

12

Interpersonal skills

Interpersonal skills

You use interpersonal skills to help you build and maintain relationships with members of your team and other people across your organisation. Creating positive relationships with them is important to your role as a business administrator as you will regularly have to work with other people to complete your tasks.

You will need to learn:

- how to use these skills to help you influence other people's opinions and views
- how to communicate your ideas and opinions effectively and respectfully
- how to challenge others appropriately, without causing conflict or upset
- how to become a role model to others, developing coaching skills to ensure that you can help others develop their own skills.

What are interpersonal skills?

> **Interpersonal skills** are skills that you use on a daily basis when interacting with other people at work and at home. They involve effectively communicating with others, listening to their opinions and views, and being able to express your own ideas to ensure that your voice is heard.

Here are some of the interpersonal skills you will need to develop while working as a business administrator.

Confidence

You must demonstrate that you have **confidence** in your own ability to fulfil your role. You need to show that, when you are allocated a task, you can complete it successfully. By communicating your confidence, others will know that you can complete the tasks they give you and that you can do this independently.

Assertiveness

At times you will need to make decisions or handle difficult conversations with others. It is important to be assertive in these situations. Assertiveness involves confidence but can also be forceful without ever becoming aggressive.

At times you may have to challenge others, either due to mistakes made or to resolve issues. You will need to push forward the decisions you have made to ensure that things get done and be assertive in sharing your decision with others, making sure you are heard and understood.

Positive work ethic

In your role, you will engage with colleagues, senior members of staff and external stakeholders, such as customers or suppliers, on a daily basis. Demonstrating a 'can do' attitude will help you have a positive work ethic. This means considering how something can be done successfully rather than highlighting reasons why things might not work. It also involves meeting deadlines. This positive approach also involves demonstrating your commitment to doing a good job and working hard to do so.

You will also need to act professionally, including your personal presentation and turning up on time to work, and communicate in an appropriate and business-like manner at all times, demonstrating your respect for others and their opinions and diversity.

Communication skills

Good communication skills are vital while working in business administration. In Chapter 13 we will discuss the different channels of communication you can use in the workplace and how you can effectively use verbal, written and digital communication. Know that how you communicate and use body language can influence how others perceive you – both inside and outside your organisation.

Key terms

Interpersonal skills – The skills used to interact and communicate with others.

Confidence – Faith in your own skills, qualities and ability.

Behaviours

Professionalism – Behaves in a professional way. This includes: personal presentation, respect, respecting and encouraging diversity to cater for wider audiences, punctuality and attitude to colleagues, customers and key stakeholders.

Personal qualities – Shows exemplary qualities that are valued including integrity, reliability, self-motivation, being proactive and a positive attitude. Motivates others where responsibility is shared.

Listening skills

Developing effective listening skills is essential. It is important to listen carefully to what other people are asking you to do to ensure that you complete the allocated task properly. You may need to ask questions to clarify what you think you have heard. You may also need to ask for information to be repeated, or for additional information, to ensure that you understand what is being asked of you.

How can you demonstrate a 'can do' attitude at work?

Demonstrating effective listening skills makes others feel that you are interested and engaged in what they have to say. Active listening can help to show that you respect others and their opinions and will help you build relationships with colleagues and other stakeholders. If people feel you are not really listening, it may make them feel undervalued and unmotivated.

To demonstrate active listening, you need to do five things.

1. Pay attention to what you are being told, avoid distractions and acknowledge what is being said.

2. Show that you are listening by using effective body language such as nodding, smiling and positioning your body towards the speaker.

3. Provide feedback on what is being said. Say that you agree (if you do agree) and make encouraging comments to ensure that the speaker continues to explain the information being provided. If you disagree, be careful not to be confrontational and maybe wait until the speaker has finished talking before commenting.

4. Don't make snap decisions or judgements. Let the speaker finish before you make a decision. They may make more relevant points or give more information that may change your mind.

5. Respond appropriately, repeating the key points that have been made to clarify your understanding and show respect for the speaker.

Empathy

Your role means you will regularly be working with and communicating with other people. Demonstrating your **empathy** involves considering other people's points of view and feelings.

You will need to think about how the other person is feeling when they are interacting with you. What emotions are they feeling? Are they anxious or worried? Upset or concerned? Considering these emotions will help you find the right way to handle the situation, using other interpersonal and communication skills to resolve issues or make effective decisions.

You should also consider what they want to get from the situation. Knowing what they want to achieve will help you consider how you can move forward and successfully complete the task or resolve the situation.

If you do not demonstrate empathy, it can make others feel that you do not care about their feelings or point of view. This can become a barrier to building positive relationships with others and may also lead to conflict.

Key term

Empathy – The ability to understand and share other people's feelings.

Challenging interpersonal skills

Some interpersonal skills may be required less often but can be challenging. In difficult situations, controlling your own emotions and being systematic in your approach will help you be effective in your role.

Negotiation skills

At times you will need to negotiate with others. This may be with other members of staff – such as when making decisions about what needs to be done and the best way to do it or when negotiating to resolve conflicts or disagreements – or it may be with customers and suppliers, such as negotiating solutions to complaints.

Negotiation is a formal discussion between people who have different aims or intentions, with the aim of reaching an agreement. You must consider how you negotiate to ensure that you achieve a successful outcome. Using a systematic process while negotiating can help you resolve the issues. Stages to consider in the negotiation process are as follows.

1. Prepare what you want to say and what needs to be discussed before you start the negotiation.

2. Discuss the issues at hand and all the information available.

3. Clarify goals so everyone is aware of what needs to be achieved.

4. Propose the solution or strategy, giving reasons for the choice of this method. If this is in a formal meeting environment, it may be appropriate for this to be done by the chair of the meeting.

5. Negotiate with each person, letting them explain their views and listen to each other respectfully.

6. Agree the strategy and outcome.

7. Implement action once you have everyone's agreement.

How can you use the negotiation process at work?

Listening to and acting on feedback

An important aspect of interpersonal skills in your role is listening to and acting on feedback. This could be feedback to help you improve your skills or advice and guidance on how to complete tasks. Table 1 shows people who may be able to give you feedback and the types of feedback they can offer.

Source of feedback	Type of feedback
Team members	These are the people who work with you most closely and are in a good position to give feedback. They can give you feedback on how something worked or your performance in your role. However, they may be biased and not always able to be neutral. Be realistic about how useful this feedback may or may not be.
Line manager	You will have a close working relationship with your line manager and they will have some responsibility for supporting you through your apprenticeship. Therefore, you can ask your line manager to give you feedback and ask them to help you find ways to improve your performance and develop your skills.
Senior management	If you have undertaken a specific task or project with senior management, they will have first-hand experience of your skills in your role and how well the task was completed.
Other teams and departments	You may be working with other teams and departments who can offer feedback on your performance and the systems in place to complete your tasks. Consider what things they can feed back on and how you can gather this feedback.
Customers	When working with customers there may be opportunities to ask them for feedback. Think about what you are going to ask and how you are going to do it. Some organisations automatically ask customers to provide feedback after you have provided your service, for example by sending a short survey.
Suppliers	You may also work with suppliers. If you do, you could ask them to provide feedback. Remember that they are busy, work in a different organisation and your request is unlikely to be a priority.
Stakeholders	Consider other stakeholders that you have interacted with. For example, you may be involved in working in the community or with other businesses in the area. Representatives of these groups could offer feedback on the service you have provided and your skills.

Table 1: Sources of feedback

Make sure you act on the feedback you have been given to improve your skills and performance or to improve the procedures used to complete the tasks that you are set.

Emotional intelligence

Being aware of your own emotions is an important skill when working with others. You have to consider **emotional intelligence** when working with other people. Emotional intelligence is about being aware of your own emotions and knowing how to control them. Ensuring that you make decisions and act without being driven by your emotions is vital, so that the actions you take are thought through properly and are the right ones.

At times you may feel upset or frustrated at work. Knowing how to control how you feel when interacting with others is key in maintaining and building relationships. You should learn how to express your emotions without causing upset or conflict with others and how to show good judgement and empathy.

Key term

Emotional intelligence – Being aware of and being able to control your own emotions.

Building and maintaining positive relationships

Building good relationships is key to the success of any organisation. The organisation needs to build trust with all its key stakeholders to ensure they can work together to achieve objectives (see Chapter 3). You will need to use all of the interpersonal skills outlined in this chapter to help you build and maintain positive relationships.

To help you build positive relationships with people within your organisation, try the following.

1. Take time to get to know people in the organisation. Taking time to introduce yourself and to find out about other people and their roles will help people recognise you and start to form a relationship.

2. Be proactive. Offer to help others and involve yourself in projects and activities. This will demonstrate that you are a team player and want to be part of the wider organisation, not just fulfil your own role.

3. Complete tasks on time and do them well. This will help people develop trust in you and let them know that you can do your job well.

4. Participate fully in meetings. Make sure that you speak up in meetings when you have something positive to offer, so that people become aware of you and trust that you have something to offer the organisation.

5. Be respectful to others. We have already discussed the importance of respect and empathy in this chapter. It is vital to demonstrate these interpersonal skills to help you develop positive relationships with others.

Once you have built positive relationships with others, it is also essential to maintain these relationships.

- Keep in touch with colleagues and catch up with them on a regular basis. This will help your colleagues remember who you are and what you do in the organisation. It may also help you develop relationships, helping to create a positive image of yourself.

- Show your appreciation for their support and assistance when colleagues help you. This will ensure that they know you value their time and effort and make them feel appreciated.

- Make sure that you offer your help and support when colleagues need it. Doing so will encourage them to trust you and come to you for help and support if they need it.

- Respect diversity. Your colleagues need to know that you respect everyone, regardless of their gender, race or ethnic background.

- Continue to be proactive and take part. Offer to participate in projects and events to help you maintain a positive image. The more that people see you contributing positively to the organisation, the more likely they are to want to involve you.

Once these positive relationships are built, your colleagues will begin to respect you and trust that you can complete the tasks that you have been set independently without interference. It will also help to ensure that your line manager knows that you are capable of producing high quality work, and therefore they may be more likely to give you more challenging and interesting jobs. This will make your job more varied and help motivate you.

What do you do to build positive relationships in your organisation?

By building and maintaining positive relationships at work, other people across the organisation will become aware of your skills and qualities. This may help you work towards promotions and may mean that you are asked to participate in interesting and exciting projects. This will help you further develop your skills and allow you to learn how to do new things.

Finally, building positive relationships at work makes teamwork and collaboration more effective. It can also make your time at work more enjoyable as you will have developed good relationships with colleagues. All of this helps to motivate and, in turn, helps you do a better job. If you build and maintain positive relationships, this can also help you avoid conflict, and support you when you are dealing with challenges that may come along.

Influencing and challenging others

Responsibility – Demonstrates taking responsibility for team performance and quality of projects delivered. Takes a clear interest in seeing that projects are successfully completed and customer requests are handled appropriately. Takes initiative to develop own and others' skills and behaviours.

You will at times need to influence and challenge others. It is important to consider when and how you will do this and how you can use your interpersonal skills to help you do it in a sensitive and effective way.

Influencing the views and decisions of others

Table 2 shows the actions and questions you should consider when attempting to influence the views and decisions of others. You may believe that a decision that is being made is not the best one for the organisation, or wish to implement a new procedure or launch a new project.

Action	Questions
Sell the idea	What are the benefits of your ideas or point of view? How will it benefit the organisation? How will it benefit the individuals you are trying to influence?
Consider the limitations	Have you considered all the limitations and negative effects? Have you got solutions to the issues so that you can convince others that you have thought it through?
Think about the time and place	Is it best to do it in a large meeting or on a one-to-one basis? Is it appropriate to do it in a busy office or would it be better somewhere quiet? Should you do it immediately, or think first and then act?
Use appropriate communication skills	Have you considered what form of communication is most appropriate? What channel should you use?

Table 2: Steps to influence others

Appropriately challenging others

You will sometimes need to challenge other people's performance, or maybe their actions towards yourself and/or others. You must do this appropriately and respectfully, while making your opinions and the reasons behind them clear. Table 3 outlines the considerations you should make before challenging someone.

Action	Considerations
Select an appropriate time and place	You will need to think about how, when and where to challenge the other person. You may need to act immediately if it is a serious issue or has a considerable impact on the organisation.
Take time to prepare and plan what you are going to say	It is important to plan in advance so that you are well prepared and know what you are going to say and how. This is especially important if you are going to challenge someone more senior to you.
Gather all the information you need in advance	Make sure that you have all the information you need at hand. You may need to gather further information and get feedback from others before you challenge the individual.
Use empathy to calm challenging situations	If you can consider the viewpoint of the other person and how they feel, you can find a way to defuse the situation and move on. Think about how you would feel if you were them and use this perspective to consider what you should do.
De-escalate conflict	If conflict arises, you will need to consider how you can de-escalate it. Under pressure, we sometimes very quickly make decisions about what to do and say. Slow down and think about your actions. This will give you time to consider all options and make a conscious decision about the best course of action.
Minimise your own negative emotional reactions	You need to act as a positive role model. Think about your own reactions and minimise your own negative emotions. You should act only on the available information and facts.
Control your own emotions in tense situations	Witnessing other people's negative emotions or conflicts is difficult. Think carefully about how your emotions and reactions will make other people feel.
Demonstrate sensitivity to other people's feelings	Demonstrating your sensitivity to other people's feelings needs to be sincere, and the other person needs to feel that you genuinely understand their feelings. Confirm how they feel before you act.

Table 3: Steps to challenge inappropriate actions

Developing coaching skills

Coaching involves working with others to help them develop their skills. They may be junior or newer colleagues who have not yet learned how to complete certain tasks. Or they could be other, more experienced members of staff who find some aspects of administration challenging, such as using IT effectively.

Coaching does not just involve showing or telling someone how to do something. It involves working with the individual to establish what they want to achieve, audit their current skills and review the different ways they can be developed. The GROW coaching model (see Figure 1) is commonly used to help people do this.

G	R	O	W
Goal	**Reality**	**Options**	**Will**
Identifies and agrees on what the individual wants to achieve.	Identify what the individual can do now, and how this is different to what they would like to be able to do.	Explore different ways in which the skills that are needed can be developed.	Decide on what will be done and put it into practice.

Figure 1: How could you use the four stages of the GROW model to coach others?

You may be asked to coach others. There are a number of interpersonal skills and personal qualities that are important when coaching others, shown in Table 4. You need to develop these skills and qualities and demonstrate that you can use them.

Interpersonal skills	Personal qualities
Communication skills	Patience
Empathy	Knowledge
Respect	Experience
Assertiveness	Tact
Listening skills	Dependability
Questioning skills	Good role model
Emotional intelligence	Trustworthy

Table 4: Interpersonal skills and personal qualities needed for coaching

Becoming a role model

A **role model** is someone who others see as setting a good example and performing well in their role.

As a role model you will:

- fulfil all aspects of your role well, producing high-quality work

- demonstrate confidence and leadership skills

- communicate effectively, interacting appropriately with others

- demonstrate concern for others

- respect others in the organisation and respect diversity

- be knowledgeable and skilled in your role

- be trustworthy and dependable

- be able to admit your mistakes and strive to improve.

Key term

Role model – A person who is looked at by others to set an example.

Summary

In this section you have learned about the key interpersonal skills that will help you thrive as a business administrator. As well as defining what interpersonal skills are, it has covered:
- building and maintaining positive relationships
- influencing and challenging others
- developing coaching skills.

Activities

▶ Activity 1: Using your interpersonal skills

Make a list of the interpersonal skills you use at work on a regular basis. Consider examples of situations where you have demonstrated using these skills to help you prepare for your end point assessment. Record your reflections in a table like the one below.

Interpersonal skill	Example	How well did I do it?

▶ Activity 2: Active listening skills

Consider a situation at work recently where you had to listen to someone else.

- How did you demonstrate active listening skills?
- What active listening skills did you use?
- What did you do well?
- How could you improve next time?

▶ Activity 3: Building and maintaining positive relationships

What have you done in your role to build and maintain positive relationships with other people in your organisation? Who are these relationships with?

Use the tips provided in this chapter to help you identify anything that you have done so far to develop these relationships. What else could you do to maintain and further develop these relationships?

▶ Activity 4: Influencing and challenging others

Reflect on a situation at work where you have needed to influence or challenge others. Make notes to answer the following.

- What was the situation?
- Who did it involve?
- What did you do?
- What went well?
- What could you have done differently to improve the outcome?

▶ Activity 5: Coaching skills

Consider the people within your organisation. Identify any individuals who might benefit from support in using business administration and IT systems. Approach these individuals to see if they would be willing for you to coach them to help develop their skills. You will need to keep a record of what you do, what coaching skills you use and how well you coached them in developing their skills. Include information on:

- who the person is
- what they needed help with
- how you organised to help them
- the coaching skills you used to help them
- what went well
- what you would do differently next time
- what feedback you received and how you could apply it.

Topic consolidation

▶ Test yourself

1. When interacting with others at work today, were you:
   - ☐ polite?
   - ☐ respectful?
   - ☐ dismissive?
   - ☐ abrupt?

2. When considering your own emotional intelligence, do you:
   - ☐ consider others' opinions of you?
   - ☐ control your own emotions?
   - ☐ reflect on your own performance?
   - ☐ slow down and make reasoned decisions?

3. When listening to others, do you:
   - ☐ listen carefully to everything they say?
   - ☐ ask questions to clarify your understanding?
   - ☐ interrupt to make corrections or share your opinion?
   - ☐ make snap decisions about what they are saying?

4. In times of conflict, are you:
   - ☐ calm and in control?
   - ☐ stressed and anxious?
   - ☐ out of your comfort zone?
   - ☐ relaxed and detached?

5. Think of a time where you had to deal with a situation of trivial conflict. Did you:
   - ☐ not intervene?
   - ☐ negotiate to achieve a resolution?
   - ☐ intervene, reporting it to your manager?
   - ☐ hold a meeting to facilitate a resolution?

6. When challenging others at work, do you:
   - ☐ take time to prepare?
   - ☐ act immediately?
   - ☐ confront others with the information you have?
   - ☐ gather all the information before acting?

7. When coaching with others, are you:
   - ☐ patient?
   - ☐ calm?
   - ☐ assertive?
   - ☐ informative?

Communication

Communication

Good communication is vital to working effectively as a business administrator. Communicating well can be difficult but will help you work well with others in the organisation to complete your daily tasks and duties. This chapter covers:

- different methods of communication
- using appropriate communication channels
- avoiding barriers to communication
- answering questions from inside and outside your organisation.

Methods of communication (1)

You need to think carefully about how you use communication to ensure that you are communicating information effectively in your role as a business administrator, with people both inside and outside your organisation. Communication involves sending and receiving information. This can be done by using **verbal communication** and **body language**, by **written communication**, or on a digital platform.

The way you communicate in a work environment is different to the way you communicate with your friends and family. It might at first feel strange communicating in a more formal way, so it is important to practise the skills involved to help you communicate in a professional manner and to represent your organisation or department well.

Communication formats

Communicating effectively depends initially on selecting the correct format. You will use three main formats of communication:

- verbal formats – e.g. face to face, telephone, conference call, recorded
- written formats – e.g. letters, reports, bulletins, posters, agendas, minutes, spreadsheets, tables, receipts, invoices, flyers
- digital formats – e.g. social media, internet, intranet.

Verbal communication

While at work, you will often communicate verbally. How you communicate verbally affects how the message is received, so it is important that you do this effectively. When communicating verbally, consider the factors shown in Figure 1.

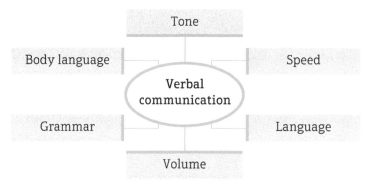

Figure 1: What types of verbal communication do you use at work?

Tone
The tone of your voice is crucial when you communicate. If you sound aggressive or bad-tempered, this can stop people listening to and understanding the message. Try not to speak in a single pitch and vary your tone to match what you are saying.

Speed
If you speak too quickly, this may cause parts of the message to be missed or misunderstood. However, talking too slowly can be frustrating for the listener and make the communication ineffective.

Language
When communicating verbally at work, it is important to use formal and professional language so that other people both within and outside the organisation recognise your professionalism. Try and avoid slang terms and jargon or technical language that others might not understand.

Volume
It is important to consider the volume at which you speak, especially when the messages you are giving include sensitive information. Talking too quietly can mean that messages are not fully received, but equally talking too loudly can be disruptive in the work environment.

Grammar
Even when communicating verbally, make sure you use correct grammar. This helps ensure the message you are communicating is professional and creates a positive image of you and your company.

Body language
Body language is significant when communicating verbally with others. Body language involves using your posture and movement to convey a message.

You need to consider how to use body language effectively to help you communicate with others inside and outside of the organisation.

- Facial expressions – frowning or smiling when talking to people makes a difference to how they interpret what you are telling them. If you want to give a serious message or instruction, it helps to have a serious facial expression at that time. If you want to appear open and approachable, smiling encourages people to want to talk to you.

- Eye contact – making eye contact with colleagues when you talk to them is important in gaining their trust and getting them to listen to what you have to say.

- Gestures – using hand gestures can help to explain what you mean and engage others in your conversation. It is also a good way of providing information quickly, for example by pointing at something to draw someone's attention to it.

Behaviours B

Professionalism – Behaves in a professional way. This includes: personal presentation, respect, respecting and encouraging diversity to cater for wider audiences, punctuality and attitude to colleagues, customers and key stakeholders.

- Posture – the way you stand or sit can help people take you seriously. If you slouch in your seat or at your desk, people may not listen to you when you offer them instructions or ask them to do something.

- Touch – you must be careful in using touch to convey a message within the workplace. Innocent or well-meant forms of encouragement, such as a pat on the back, could be misconstrued as unwanted attention.

What body language are you conscious of using?

Methods of communication (2)

Written communication

As a business administrator you need to ensure that you communicate effectively with others to fulfil your role. You will be expected to produce records and documents to a high quality. Additionally, you may be expected to coach others within the workplace to develop their skills in written communication. The written formats that you may use include:

- letters to customers, potential members of staff, suppliers, etc.

- emails to other members of staff, suppliers, members of the public, etc.

- reports or proposals produced for other members of staff to provide information or updates

- presentations to update members of staff or your organisation's directors, or to introduce new initiatives

- minutes of meetings to record the discussions held and decisions made

- spreadsheets and databases to record and analyse data.

You will need to practise producing documents and records to ensure that your skills in written communication are effective and to provide evidence for your portfolio interview as part of your end point assessment. See Chapter 9 for a reminder about using IT to create these documents and Chapter 10.

Consider the following when communicating in a written format.

- **Selection of software/format** – make sure you select the most appropriate software to produce the document. Create an appropriate structure to help the reader understand the information provided.

- **Corporate image and style** – some forms of written communication, such as a report, may have a specific format; it is important that you follow your organisation's format to ensure continuity of the company's corporate image and brand.

- **Spelling, punctuation and grammar** – you will also need to check spelling, punctuation and grammar in written communications to make sure that the message is clear and there are no errors.

- **Providing clear information and a clear message** – when communicating in writing, it is important that the message and the information is clear to the receiver. If it isn't, then there is the potential for misunderstanding, errors and potential upset or offence.

- **Using appropriate language and tone** – you need to consider your tone and the language you use, so that you convey a professional image to others inside and outside your organisation.

Behaviours B

Professionalism – Behaves in a professional way. This includes: personal presentation, respect, respecting and encouraging diversity to cater for wider audiences, punctuality and attitude to colleagues, customers and key stakeholders.

Methods of communication (3)

Digital communication

You may also use digital communication in your role as a business administrator. The basic underlying principles are the same as for verbal communication and written communication, but there are some other things to consider, too.

Digital communication includes platforms that you may already be familiar with but there are likely to be others specific to your organisation.

- **Videos** – videos can be used to provide information to staff on procedures such as fire safety or to customers to promote the organisation's products or services. You may contribute to the production of videos. You may even use short video clips to help others improve their IT skills.

- **Internet** – you will use the internet regularly in your role. This may be to undertake research to support the organisation or to update information about the organisation, such as in online directories. Remember that your internet use should be work-related during office hours.

- **Websites** – your organisation will have its own website and you may need to provide information for the website to keep it up to date.

- **Intranet** – your organisation will have its own internal network or intranet. This is where internal information is shared with staff.

- **Mobile phones and apps** – organisations often use smartphone technology and apps to keep people up to date with important information and to communicate with customers. You need to consider what information is appropriate to be communicated in this way.

- **Social media** – social media such as Facebook, Twitter and Instagram is increasingly used by organisations to market their products and services. You may have your own profiles, where you post information about yourself. Remember that any information you post about yourself could be seen by the general public, so you need to think carefully about what you post and how it reflects on you. Any negative images, messages or information about you could reflect badly on the organisation you work for.

Choosing the right communication format

There are advantages and disadvantages of using each of the three formats, shown in Table 1. You need to consider these before using them in the workplace.

Format	Advantages	Disadvantages
Verbal	Saves time Flexible Creates a **rapport**	Emotions can distort the message Not recorded Easy to forget the message
Written	Provides a record Easy to present complex information Formal image created	Expensive Time consuming Delay in response
Digital	Cost effective Widespread audience Convenient	Can become outdated Text-based so can exclude some people Information overload

Table 1: Advantages and disadvantages of the communication formats

Factors that affect the choice of communication media

When deciding which communication format to use, there are a number of factors and questions that you need to consider.

- Audience – how large/small, near/far/dispersed, etc. are the intended recipients?

- Purpose – is the purpose, nature and tone of the communication **formal**, **informal**, critical or routine?

- Cost – what is the most cost-efficient way of transmitting the information to the intended recipients?

- Speed – how urgently should the information be transmitted and received?

- Subject matter – how complex, or commercially valuable or sensitive, is the communication?

- Amount or volume – how much information is there to be transmitted?

- Feedback – do you require a direct response from the recipient?

- Record – do you need a record of the communication to provide evidence of it taking place?

- Intrusion – how intrusive or disruptive is the communication method?

Key terms

Rapport – A close relationship where people understand each other's feelings or ideas and communicate well.

Formal communication – Communication through the organisation's official channels.

Informal communication – Communication through unofficial channels such as rumours, gossip and chats at the coffee machine.

The communication process

Any communication you undertake involves the same process, shown in Table 2. The message is sent from the source to the recipient using an appropriate communication channel. However, some barriers to communication (sometimes called 'noise') can get in the way, making the communication less effective. You need to understand how the communication process works and how to avoid the noise to help you communicate in the best way possible.

Source	The source initiates the conversation.
Message	The source decides on the message and the channel to be used.
Encoding	The source uses communication and, if appropriate, body language to send the information as a message.
Channel	The source chooses the communication – verbal, written or digital format.
Receiver	The receiver is the person who the message is intended for.
Decoding	The receiver interprets the message and tries to understand it.
Feedback	Feedback is the final step, when the receiver sends information back to the source and vice versa.
Noise	The noise is the barrier to communication that may get in the way of the messages being received and understood.

Table 2: The stages of communication

Communication needs and requirements

Before you communicate with others, consider the purpose of the communication. Is it to pass on instructions quickly to a colleague or to gather their ideas for a new project? Is it to engage with a customer who lives on the other side of the world? The purpose of the communication will help you consider the appropriate communication method to use.

In some organisations you may find that there are policies and processes in place requiring you to communicate in a certain way. For example, if you need to communicate with other members of staff to organise a meeting, your employer may require you to do this in a written format, such as an email outlining the agenda items.

You also need to consider the language you use. Your employer will expect you to be professional at all times and to use language that is appropriate for the workplace. You need to remember that at all times at work you are representing your employer or department and you must consider the language you use. Sometimes, not thinking about the way we phrase instructions, ideas or feedback can upset other people and this could mean that you harm the working relationship you have with other members of staff.

Customers have expectations of the company you work for and you will need to make sure you meet these expectations at all times, especially when responding to questions. Customers will expect you to be polite and welcoming when you communicate with them, so you need to practise to ensure that you communicate appropriately with customers.

Communication channels

Communication is passed through a number of different channels in any organisation. You need to be able to identify the different communication channels in your organisation and learn to communicate appropriately in each channel.

Direct communication

This occurs when a message is transmitted from its source (the organisation) directly through a distribution channel to the receiver without anyone else involved or any noise. Examples include emails, letters or in person through face-to-face meetings.

Indirect communication

This occurs when a message is transmitted from the source through another person or organisation to the receiver. There is a risk here that the intermediary person could misinterpret or misrepresent the information and the message will not be clear or accurate when it is received.

Chain of command

Communication is passed through the chain of command up and down the hierarchy. This is where information is cascaded down from senior management into teams and vice versa.

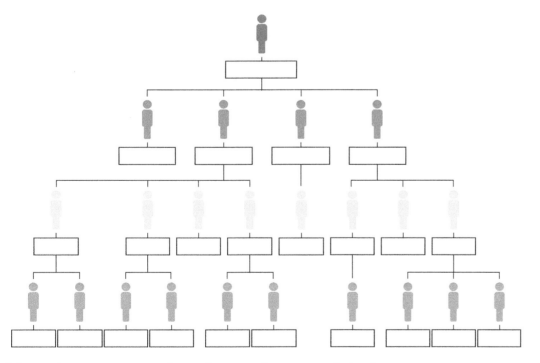

What is the communication chain of command in your workplace?

Barriers to communication (1)

You will encounter barriers to communication or 'noise'. To ensure that you communicate well with others in the organisation and create good relationships, you will need to identify potential barriers to communication and find ways to overcome them. The barriers are summarised in Figure 2.

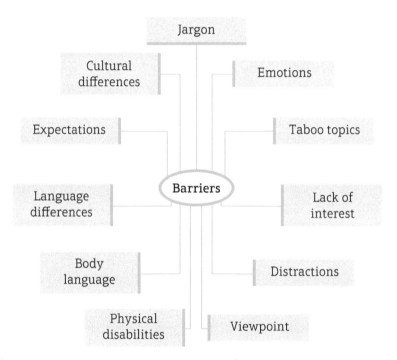

Figure 2: What barriers to communication might you face in your role?

Use of jargon

Using technical language or terms, commonly known as 'jargon', when communicating could be confusing, especially if you are answering customers' questions. Before you communicate, think about what words the recipient will understand and explain any technical terms in order to ensure that they understand you.

Emotions

If you or others are feeling stressed or upset, your message may get distorted or misunderstood. Be aware of your own and others' emotions and consider the best way to communicate the message without causing offence. This is especially true if you are answering questions from outside the organisation, such as from an upset customer or client.

Taboo topics

Sometimes the topic you need to discuss will be sensitive or one that people are uncomfortable discussing. You will need to think carefully about how to introduce the topic. Consider finding somewhere quiet, away from others, to help the recipient feel comfortable.

Lack of interest or relevance

Even though you may understand the importance or relevance of the message, others may not be as interested. They may consider the information you are sharing to be irrelevant to them. Take time to consider what they need to know and remove anything unnecessary.

Distraction

In the workplace there are distractions that can get in the way of communicating effectively with other members of staff. Move the conversation to a quieter area to minimise distractions. Before you start a conversation, make sure that you and the recipient are able to give it your full attention.

Perception and viewpoint

Others will not always share your viewpoint and may perceive something in a different way. You need to consider differing viewpoints and either change their point of view or explain that, while they may disagree, you are still taking the action that you feel is right.

Physical disabilities

Some of the people you work with or customers may have hearing or speech impairments. In this instance, you must think about how best to communicate. Similarly, if the colleague or customer is blind, written or digital communication may need to be adapted. Either way, checking that they have understood the message may help ensure effective communication.

Body language

Inappropriate body language prevents effective communication. Consider what your body language says to the person you are talking to. Does it say that you are interested or bored? Do you seem aggressive or too laid back? Remember that different cultures have different ways of interpreting the same body language.

Language differences

Some people may have English as a second language. You will need to plan for this and consider how you will overcome the language barrier.

Expectations and prejudices

We can have preconceived ideas about colleagues and customers, and have expectations and prejudices that get in the way of communicating effectively. Treat everyone with the same respect and consideration. Do not assume something about someone or confine them to a stereotype.

Cultural differences

If you work internationally or with people from different cultures, some differences may get in the way of effective communication. Develop your cultural awareness of different values and behaviours and act accordingly.

Behaviours B

Adaptability – Is able to accept and deal with changing priorities related to both their own work and to the organisation.

Barriers to communication (2)

Methods to overcome barriers to communication

Once you have identified potential or actual barriers to communication, you need to find ways to avoid them. Here are some tips to consider.

- Focus on the receiver and avoid distractions.

- Take the receiver and their needs seriously.

- Give a crystal-clear message – practise it in advance if that helps.

- Consider the technique used to deliver the message to ensure that it is skilfully delivered.

- Use multiple channels to deliver the message so that you know it is received and understood.

- Be aware of and control your own emotions and attitudes.

- Understand and prepare for the needs and background of the audience.

- Use the seven Cs of communication, which are outlined in the next section.

How do you communicate information to others at work?

Seven Cs of communication

The seven Cs of communication, shown in Figure 3, can help you communicate effectively.

*   **Clarity** – be clear about the goal or purpose of your communication.
*   **Credibility** – ensure information that you communicate is reliable, trustworthy and dependable.
*   **Content** – only include content that is relevant and meaningful to what is being said.
*   **Context** – consider the background and wider meanings of what is being said.
*   **Continuity** – connect information in a logical, consistent and continuous manner.
*   **Capability** – ensure that the recipients have the power or ability to do what is being asked of them.
*   **Channels** – communicate using channels appropriate to the message.

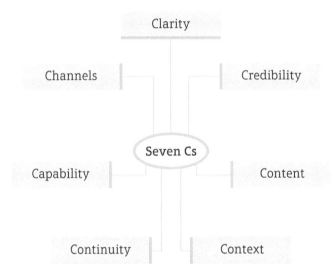

Figure 3: How can using the seven Cs of communication help you communicate more effectively?

Impacts of ineffective communication

Ineffective or poor communication can have a serious impact on your organisation and make it more difficult for you to fulfil your role.

*   **Increased errors and mistakes** – if members of staff do not understand what to do and how to do it, they will make errors. This can waste time and money, as well as having a negative effect on customers.
*   **Poor decision making** – if people misunderstand messages or lack important information, they can make decisions that may not be the best for the organisation.
*   **Conflict and disagreement** – poor communication can lead to conflicts and disagreement at work, preventing the job being done effectively. You need to ensure that you work to resolve any issues that arise but try to avoid them in the first place.

- **Misunderstandings and confusion** – when communication is not clear, it leads to misunderstandings and confusion, which slows down tasks.
- **Lower efficiency** – if people constantly have to check messages and ask for clarification, this can lead to inefficiency.
- **Decreased employee morale** – poor communication can be demotivating for employees and may mean they are less willing to work well for the organisation.

Handling queries and answering questions

While working as a business administrator, you will be expected to handle queries and answer questions. These may be from colleagues and others within the organisation, or from people outside the business. It is important that you develop good communication skills to help you answer questions effectively, ensuring that you understand the question asked and provide an answer which is clear and complete. You will need to consider the following when handling queries and answering questions.

- Listen carefully to the question asked, making sure that you make a note of any important information provided.
- Ask further questions to ensure that you fully understand what is being asked of you.
- Clarify anything that you are not sure about by restating the question asked and asking if the information you have is correct.
- Think carefully about your answer before answering the question. If you need time to consider the answer, then tell the person asking the question that you need some more time and that you will get back to them.
- If you are not sure of the answer, you may need to look it up or ask someone else for assistance. It is better to check that the information is correct before you offer it, rather than rush and get things wrong.
- Once you have answered the question/handled the query, check that you have covered everything the person was asking for, asking if they need anything more.

Remember that when answering questions and handling queries you are representing your organisation and therefore you will need to present a professional and business-like image of yourself. Think carefully about the language and tone you use and ensure that you work within your organisation's policies and procedures.

Summary

In this section you have learned about the different methods of communication, how to use communication effectively, how to identify communication channels and barriers to communication, and how to overcome them. This section has covered:
- verbal (including body language), written and digital formats of communication
- factors affecting your communication media choice
- the communication process and communication channels
- communication needs and requirements
- the effect of ineffective communication
- handling and answering queries.

Activities

▶ **Activity 1: Verbal communication**

Create a table to outline the people you have spoken with recently at work. Were they positive or negative experiences?

If you are using an online portfolio you could also, with permission, create an image of your working environment and the policies and procedures you work around.

▶ **Activity 2: Written communication**

Think of a situation recently when you have had to communicate in a written format. This could have been a letter, a report, a proposal or a presentation, for example.

- What software did you use?
- What format did you produce?
- What did you do well?
- What did you do less well?
- What can you do to improve next time?

▶ **Activity 3: Digital communication**

Carry out research into how your organisation uses digital communication. Summarise your research in a table like the one below.

Digital communication	Use	Internal/ external	Positive effects	Negative effects

---

▶ **Activity 4: Barriers to communication**

Make a list of barriers to communication that could occur – or have occurred – while you are working in your role as a business administrator. For each of the barriers, suggest some solutions, explaining how you could/have overcome them in your role.

You may find this useful evidence for your portfolio interview.

Topic consolidation

▶ Test yourself

1. Today were you:
   - ☐ happy?
   - ☐ sad?
   - ☐ indifferent?
   - ☐ grumpy?

2. When answering questions at work, do you:
   - ☐ answer straight away?
   - ☐ refer the answer to someone else?
   - ☐ take time to consider the answer?
   - ☐ make up the answer?

3. When communicating verbally at work today, were you:
   - ☐ polite?
   - ☐ assertive?
   - ☐ professional?
   - ☐ quiet?

4. When you use social media, do you:
   - ☐ post about your social life?
   - ☐ consider how the information reflects on you?
   - ☐ think about the impact on your job role?
   - ☐ only post direct messages to your friends?

5. When communicating with a colleague, were you:
   - ☐ positive?
   - ☐ negative?
   - ☐ assertive?
   - ☐ passive?

6. When handling a challenging conversation, do you:
   - ☐ listen to others' points of view?
   - ☐ assume the issues involved?
   - ☐ dominate the conversation?
   - ☐ respond immediately to the issues?

7. When having a meeting, were you:
   - ☐ under pressure because of time constraints?
   - ☐ unsure of your role?
   - ☐ clear when setting expectations?
   - ☐ distracted by other aspects of your role?

14

Quality

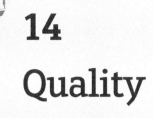

Quality

The quality of the work done by an organisation's employees or the products produced by the organisation reflects the standard and quality of the organisation itself. When things don't live up to expectations, the way that challenging complaints are dealt with requires problem-solving skills to ensure standards and quality get back on track.

Completing tasks to a high standard

Behaviours

Professionalism – Behaves in a professional way. This includes: personal presentation, respect, respecting and encouraging diversity to cater for wider audiences, punctuality and attitude to colleagues, customers and key stakeholders.

Personal qualities – Shows exemplary qualities that are valued including integrity, reliability, self-motivation, being proactive and a positive attitude. Motivates others where responsibility is shared.

Responsibility – Demonstrates taking responsibility for team performance and quality of projects delivered. Takes a clear interest in seeing that projects are successfully completed and customer requests handled appropriately. Takes initiative to develop own and others' skills and behaviours.

The workplace is a busy environment and at times you will feel overstretched. Even when this happens, it is important to complete your tasks to a high standard.

Never agree to impossible deadlines

It might be tempting to agree to a deadline because you do not want to say 'no' but it is important not to over-commit your time. If you know that it will be impossible to complete a task within the timescales you have been given, then you should explain why you cannot achieve the task by then and negotiate a realistic deadline.

Once you have agreed or negotiated a new deadline, it is important that you meet it. If you think that the deadline will not be met, then you should raise this as soon as possible.

Plan how you will complete the task

Planning how you will complete the task will improve your efficiency. Identify any resources that you may need, the people you may need to speak to or to assist you, and allocate time when you can work on the task.

Manage your time

Time management is key. If you have planned to work on a task at a specific time, then ensure that you do. If necessary, move away from your usual work area so that you cannot be disturbed or, if this is not possible, let your colleagues know that you should not be disturbed. Turn on your phone's voicemail and close your email program.

Managing yourself is key to time management. Keep all distractions to a minimum and gather all the resources you need before you start. Give yourself regular breaks and, if possible, take these breaks away from your work area. Be disciplined about returning to your task when your break is over.

Concentrate and focus on the task

Stay focused by concentrating on the task you are completing. Where a task has several parts, write a 'to do' list so that you can organise each of the components and concentrate on one component at a time.

Know what your organisation's standards are

What is the acceptable standard for work within your organisation? Ensure that you meet the minimum standard and where possible exceed it. Take ownership of the task and work to the best of your ability.

Check your work

Before submitting your work, ensure that it is correct. Check for accuracy of spelling, grammar and any calculations. Review each stage of the task. If it is written work, make sure each stage makes sense and there are no omissions. If it is a practical task, check the quality of the work at each stage you have completed. If appropriate, ask a colleague to check your work and give you feedback before making any improvements.

How can you ensure that you complete your tasks to a high standard?

Demonstrating the necessary level of expertise

In your business administration role, you need to demonstrate the right level of expertise to get your tasks done. This expertise can be developed by checking the level of expertise required then undergoing training to develop your skills and continuously improve your work.

Job description

Your job description will list any specific skills your role requires, as well as any formal qualifications needed. Job descriptions can change as organisational requirements evolve to keep up with the demands of your industry or sector. It is important that you ensure that your skills are appropriate and current. You can identify any development required and then plan to update your skills and/or knowledge.

Appraisal

Your appraisal is an ideal opportunity to discuss with your manager your current skills and how they match the demands of your job. Any **anomalies** can be identified and a plan established for you to obtain the expertise required to complete your tasks.

Personal development plan (PDP)

Your job description and appraisal can combine with self-assessment to help you identify any skills and knowledge gaps. You can then update your personal development plan (PDP), which will be part of your organisation's process for developing and up-skilling its workforce. Your PDP should focus on the skills and knowledge required to do your job, as well as identifying your future goals and ambitions.

Your PDP will often outline potential training and continuing professional development (CPD) that you can undertake to help develop your skills.

- **Training** can take many forms, from formal classroom-based training through to on-the-job training where you learn from your colleagues. Training is used to teach you how to do something, such as a specific task or how to use a piece of equipment.

- **Continuing professional development** (CPD) is more wide-ranging than training. It can involve developing transferable skills such as presentation skills or accountancy knowledge, as well as background reading done to ensure that your knowledge is kept up to date and reflects current practice in your organisation's sector.

Behaviours **B**

Managing performance – Takes responsibility for their own work, accepts feedback in a positive way, uses initiative and shows resilience. Also takes responsibility for their own development, knows when to ask questions to complete a task and informs their line manager when a task is complete. Performs thorough self-assessments of their work and complies with the organisation's procedures.

Key term

Anomalies – Things that are not standard, normal or expected.

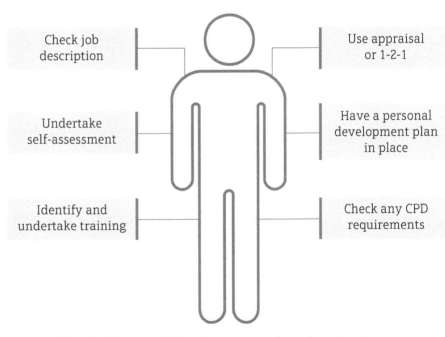

Figure 1: Which of these activities do you regularly undertake to improve your skills and knowledge?

Check job description

Use appraisal or 1-2-1

Undertake self-assessment

Have a personal development plan in place

Identify and undertake training

Check any CPD requirements

Reviewing processes and suggesting improvements

Your organisation's processes were covered in Chapter 7. They are likely to include ones for checking the quality of work or the standard of finished products.

Carrying out quality-control processes may make you think about how effective other processes are, ones that are carried out at an earlier stage. For instance, if you are checking finished products and the same issue regularly crops up, this may make you think about the product's manufacturing process.

Being able to review processes **autonomously** will demonstrate your ability to work independently and to identify areas for improvement. Any improvements you suggest must be justified so that your organisation can see the benefits.

Identify the process

The right process needs to be identified before it can be reviewed. In some organisations it may be policy to update and review processes regularly, whereas in other organisations processes may have been in place for a long time and be outdated and/or not reflect current 'best practice'. If you are reviewing a number of processes, focus first on those that are most out of date.

Discuss with immediate team

Although you may be working autonomously, you should consult with others to obtain feedback on the process you are reviewing. This is likely to include your colleagues, peers and managers. There may be key stakeholders in other departments or external to your organisation where obtaining feedback would also be useful.

Map the current process

Visualise the process by completing a 'road map' of the current process. Identify steps within the process, who is involved, what resources are required, etc. This will help you to identify the parts of the process that need improvement or updating and the parts that work well and can be transferred into a new version of the process.

Review each step of the current process

There may be steps within the current process that work well and that you may wish to keep. As you review each step, justify your decision to either keep or remove the step. How will this improve the process? What benefits will there be to the organisation?

Set the new measures for success

You need to establish that any changes made will be an improvement on the existing process. Setting measures for success and identifying how these will be implemented is key in helping you to justify the changes you are suggesting.

Key term

Autonomously – Freedom to act independently.

Behaviours

Responsibility – Demonstrates taking responsibility for team performance and quality of projects delivered. Takes a clear interest in seeing that projects are successfully completed and customer requests handled appropriately. Takes initiative to develop own and others' skills and behaviours.

Map the new process

You should map out the new process in a similar way to how you mapped out the old process. By doing this you will be able to identify any gaps in the new process and work to remove them.

Test the new process

Testing the new process will help confirm whether it is an improvement on the old one and whether you need to make any necessary tweaks. The test should be undertaken in a real work situation and with the people who will carry out the process.

Make the suggestion

Once you are confident that the new process is an improvement and can justify the change, make your recommendation to your line manager or project manager.

Document and implement the new process

You will need to document the new process so that it can be implemented across the organisation. This version should replace the old version and be stored so it is accessible, such as in the company manual/handbook or electronically on the company intranet or hard drive.

Behaviours

Adaptability – Is able to accept and deal with changing priorities related to both their own work and to the organisation.

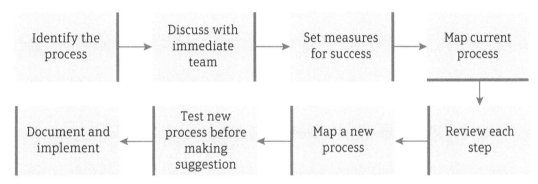

Figure 2: Which quality-control processes are you responsible for reviewing?

Sharing administrative best practice

Recognising and sharing best practice is a good way to improve the performance of others across your organisation. This can lead to the whole workforce working at a higher level as the best practice is repeated across the organisation, helping to improve quality.

To share best practice, you first need to demonstrate it. This can be through your behaviour and the standard of the work you produce, so that you actively promote your organisation's standards and best practice. Accuracy in your record keeping is an example of how you can promote and share best practice. This can coach others to work to the same quality standard by setting an example.

There are several coaching models that you can use to structure the way in which you coach and communicate the requirements for work. The GROW, CLEAR and FUEL models were covered in Chapter 10. When using these models, there are techniques you can use to make them more effective.

1. Take five minutes for a check-in in advance of the coaching session. You may use this to gather your thoughts, or to ask your coachee to write down what they want to get from the coaching session.

2. Ensure that objectives set as a result of the coaching are SMART (specific, measurable, achievable, realistic and timely).

3. Ask open-ended questions (based on 'Who ...?', 'What ...?', 'Why ...?' and 'When ...?') to allow the coachee to explore the options available to them and discuss any fears and/or anxieties they may have when learning new things.

4. Write things down. Ensure any actions that are agreed are written down, with specific details of how objectives will be met and their agreed deadlines.

5. Remain present and focused. When you are coaching, ensure that you are focused on your coachee and use active listening skills, such as nodding your head or repeating back to them key points.

6. Ask the coachee to let you know what they got out of the coaching session and what the best part was for them.

7. Arrange a follow up. Coaching is likely to be over a period of time, so arrange a follow up at the end of each session so that you can discuss progression and the achievements of your coachee.

8. Journaling. It might be appropriate for your coachee to write a journal of their progress and achievements. You can suggest this, if appropriate.

9. Actions. It may be appropriate to set small actions between coaching sessions where the coachee can work towards their final objectives or goals.

10. Coaching models. Practise using each coaching model and then use the one that you find most comfortable and is most effective with those you coach.

Which model of coaching have you used?

Resolving challenging or complex complaints

Understanding how to solve problems will help you to resolve challenging and/or complex complaints. You may be resolving internal or external situations. For example, you may have to resolve complaints from your colleagues or from another department, or you may be dealing with customers or suppliers. Whatever the situation, having the right skills to resolve challenging or complex complaints will help you to be confident in dealing with them.

When resolving challenging or complex complaints, there are five basic steps you need to follow.

1. **Define the problem** – investigate the situation so that you can be sure that you are dealing with the source of the problem rather than a symptom. For example, a supplier may be complaining that your organisation is not meeting the obligations of a contract. When you investigate, you find that there is a block in the communication channels and the invoices are not reaching your accounts department.

2. **Generate alternatives** – look for alternatives that will lead to the resolution of the complaint before taking any action. Run through each scenario to see which is likely to be most suitable and which may just create other issues or complaints. Seek the advice of other people who may be able to give feedback and offer additional alternatives.

3. **Evaluate and select an alternative** – once you have gone through each scenario, evaluate which alternative is likely to give the most satisfying results in resolving the complaint.

4. **Implement the solution** – be instrumental in ensuring that the solution is implemented efficiently and within the timescales that have been agreed.

5. **Check that all parties are happy with the solution** – once the complaint has been resolved, check that the person who made the complaint is satisfied with the resolution and that no further actions are required or expected.

Being a key point of contact for addressing issues

In your role as a business administrator you are likely to be a key point of contact for addressing any issues and complaints. You should approach any issues with a 'can do' attitude and make yourself available to those who have any complaints. With external complaints, you are representing your organisation; with internal complaints, you will be representing your department or team.

Behaviours

Professionalism – Behaves in a professional way. This includes: personal presentation, respect, respecting and encouraging diversity to cater for wider audiences, punctuality and attitude to colleagues, customers and key stakeholders.

Responsibility – Demonstrates taking responsibility for team performance and quality of projects delivered. Takes a clear interest in seeing that projects are successfully completed and customer requests handled appropriately. Takes initiative to develop own and others' skills and behaviours.

It is important to maintain a professional approach and be proactive, using several skills.

1. **Patience** – listen to the complaint and try to understand the issues that the person has and what they are looking for in the resolution.

2. **Attentiveness** – give the person your individual attention and let them know that you are doing everything possible to resolve their complaint. Look for what they are trying to say but not telling you.

3. **Clear communication** – get to the point as quickly as possible and be clear in your messages. If the person making the complaint is making unreasonable demands, you need to keep things realistic. Tell them the reasons why the resolution may not be what they expect. Keep them informed with progress and, if you foresee any delays, communicate this clearly.

What approach do you take when addressing issues?

4. **Knowledge** – having knowledge of systems and procedures will help you deal with any issues. If you are not familiar with a process, find out about it as soon as you can. It may be that you need to have knowledge of products or services. Try to predict questions that the person may have around systems, processes, products and/or services so that you can be prepared with the appropriate knowledge to be able to address their issues.

5. **Positive language** – always use language and a tone of voice that is positive as it is likely to affect the way in which the person hears what you are saying or doing.

6. **Time management** – be organised and manage your time in order to meet any deadlines and promises made. Don't put off actions that you can do immediately and be proactive in finding solutions.

Summary

In this section you have learned about different aspects of maintaining quality within your role in order to contribute to the overall quality of your organisation. It has covered:

- completing tasks to a high standard
- demonstrating the necessary level of expertise
- applying yourself to continuously improving your performance at work
- reviewing processes autonomously and making suggestions for improvements
- sharing good practice and coaching others
- applying problem-solving skills and being a key point of contact for addressing issues.

Activities

▶ Activity 1: Completing tasks to a high standard

Go through your 'things to do' list and identify tasks that require a minimum standard, then make a list of these tasks and answer the following questions.

- What deadlines will you need to set, or have you set?
- What plan is in place to complete the task?
- How will you manage your time?
- Do you need to include any contingencies?
- How will you ensure that you can concentrate on the task?
- What company standard will you adhere to?
- Who can you ask to check your work?

▶ Activity 2: Demonstrating the necessary level of expertise to complete tasks

Undertake research to establish the level of expertise required for you to complete your given tasks at work. Where can you find information of the level of expertise you require? List these documents.

Complete a self-assessment to determine if you have the expertise and skills required at the appropriate level. Ask others for feedback on your level of expertise and skills. Compare this with your self-assessment.

What evidence do you have to prove that you have the necessary level of expertise to complete your tasks at work?

▶ Activity 3: Applying yourself to continuously improve at work

Create a personal development plan or update your existing one with any personal development needs you have identified in Activity 2 above. Include:

- a self-assessment of where you are now
- feedback from others (colleagues and/or line manager)
- what you wish to achieve to ensure you have the necessary level of expertise to complete your tasks
- objectives to meet what you want to achieve
- action points to meet the objectives
- deadlines
- training and other learning opportunities available to you.

▶ Activity 4: Reviewing processes

Identify a process within your organisation that requires reviewing. Discuss the process with your team and/or line manager. Map the current process. Review each step of the current process and involve your team in this.

Set measures of success for the new process. Test the new process.

Make your suggestions. Document and implement the new process.

Topic consolidation

▶ Test yourself

1. A good way to ensure that I complete tasks to a high standard is to:
   - ☐ keep to my deadlines, even if there is no time to check my work.
   - ☐ manage myself and my time.
   - ☐ multi-task by doing several jobs at the same time.
   - ☐ agree to deadlines; even if I can't meet them, I will work it out somehow.

2. I can find out what is an appropriate level of expertise for my role by:
   - ☐ looking at my job description.
   - ☐ undertaking training.
   - ☐ drawing up a personal development plan.
   - ☐ looking at my organisation's intranet.

3. I can improve my skills at work by:
   - ☐ having a job description.
   - ☐ never having any time off.
   - ☐ having regular meetings with my team.
   - ☐ agreeing a personal development plan with my manager.

4. It is important to justify any suggestions for improvements when reviewing processes so that:
   - ☐ my organisation can see the benefits to the changes.
   - ☐ I can justify my job.
   - ☐ the processes are updated regardless of whether change is needed.
   - ☐ the workforce is kept informed.

5. Sharing quality-control best practice in my administrative role is important because:
   - ☐ it is in my job description.
   - ☐ it is likely to improve performance of others in my organisation.
   - ☐ it is a part of my personal development plan.
   - ☐ my manager is observing me to ensure that I am doing this.

6. When I am coaching others, it is important that I:
   - ☐ disregard any coaching models.
   - ☐ avoid writing anything down as anything discussed is confidential.
   - ☐ ask closed questions so that I can get exact answers from the coachee.
   - ☐ remain present and focused throughout the coaching session.

7. Defining the problem when dealing with a complaint will allow me to:
   - ☐ explain to the person complaining that it is not my organisation's fault.
   - ☐ know exactly what I am dealing with, so that I can look at alternative solutions.
   - ☐ know exactly what I am dealing with, so that I can choose whether to deal with the complaint.
   - ☐ pass the complaint on to someone else.

8. The following skill will help me when being a key point of contact for addressing issues.
   - ☐ Ability to be patient
   - ☐ Physical agility
   - ☐ Language skills
   - ☐ Computer programming skills

Planning and organisation

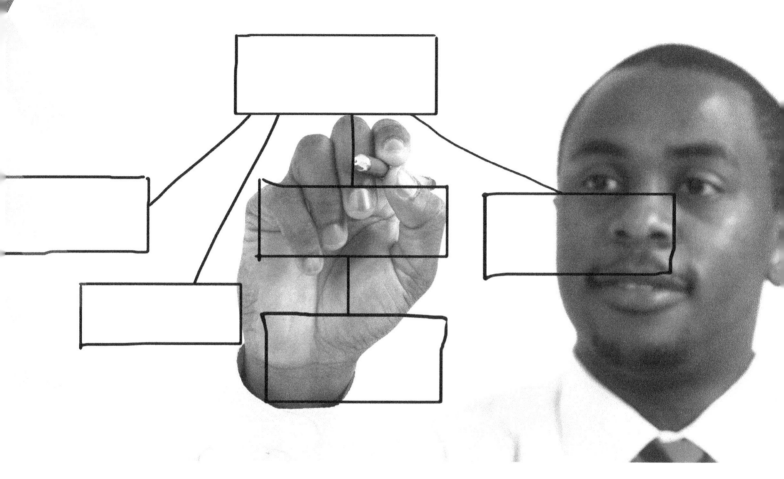

Planning and organisation

To be effective in your role as a business administrator, you need to be organised and plan how you will do things – for both your day-to-day tasks and one-off larger projects. Being organised and planning will help you take a positive and proactive approach in each of your tasks.

Taking responsibility for initiating and completing tasks

In your role as a business administrator you may be required to start or initiate tasks and projects. To do this, you need to take a proactive approach by recognising which tasks need to be done and by when.

Table 1 details techniques you can use to take responsibility for initiating and completing tasks.

Technique	How you can work on the technique
Be interested in your work	Having a genuine interest in your work helps your motivation for starting and completing tasks. Some tasks will be more interesting than others. When you need to complete a task that isn't appealing, think of the result and the benefits this will bring to you and/or your organisation.
Don't blame others for mistakes or failures	You will make mistakes sometimes. It is important that you take responsibility for these. Remain positive and seek solutions to overcome them; be confident and speak to your manager for guidance.
Ensure you meet deadlines	When beginning a new task, be realistic about deadlines. If you are working to somebody else's deadlines, negotiate dates before you start. Never agree to a deadline that you know will be impossible to meet. Effective time management will help you to meet deadlines.
Embrace challenging tasks and projects	Some tasks you undertake may stretch your skills and expertise. Embrace these challenges and identify the support you may need. Speak to your manager and negotiate additional training, if needed.
Be prepared to take risks	Assess the level of risk that may be involved and communicate this clearly to those who are involved, such as colleagues or your line manager. Think about 'what if' scenarios and have contingency plans in place.
Take the initiative	Constantly search for new solutions or more effective approaches to your tasks at work. Do more than is required of you and think of yourself as a team member rather than an employee. Always look out for new opportunities and be prepared to act.
Avoid making excuses	If you have made a mistake or a task has failed, or you have not been able to meet a deadline, be open and honest, clearly communicating the reasons why. Notify the relevant people as soon as you can and look for alternative solutions to address the issues.

Table 1: Ways to take responsibility for tasks

Managing priorities

When you have many tasks that are all important, it can be difficult to know which are the most important and which you should do first. There are several techniques you can use to order your tasks.

Speak to your manager

If you are struggling to prioritise your tasks, ask your line manager for help. They will help you work out which are the most urgent tasks and which tasks you can put to one side for the moment.

When your line manager is unavailable, who can you ask for help?

Ask others

If your tasks involve colleagues or customers, find out when they need the task completed. You may be able to **defer** certain tasks if they are not required immediately. However, these tasks will eventually become urgent as the agreed deadline approaches. You must therefore ensure that you allow enough time in the future to complete the task.

Work backwards

Review when each task is due to be completed. You can then estimate how much time each task is likely to need to complete and see which to prioritise accordingly – if a task will take more time, then it might be more urgent even than one that needs to be finished sooner.

Manage expectations

Once you have prioritised your tasks, work out the order in which you will complete them and the dates by which they are likely to be achieved. Communicate this schedule to those involved. Letting the individuals know when the work will be done will help to manage their expectations.

Behaviours

Managing performance – Takes responsibility for their own work, accepts feedback in a positive way, uses initiative and shows resilience. Also takes responsibility for their own development, knows when to ask questions to complete a task and informs their line manager when a task is complete. Performs thorough self-assessments of their work and complies with the organisation's procedures.

Key term

Defer – To put off or postpone an action or event until a later time.

Managing time

Once you have prioritised your tasks, you need to work out how you will complete them within the timescales set. Managing your time is crucial to stay on target and help you meet your deadlines.

Distinguish between urgent and important tasks

Evaluate each of your tasks and decide whether it is urgent and/or important. Once you have done this you can put them into a table similar to the one shown in Table 2. This will show you if the tasks are urgent and important, important but not urgent, not important but urgent, or not urgent and not important.

	Urgent	Not urgent
Important	Urgent and important	Important but not urgent
Not important	Urgent but not important	Not urgent and not important

Table 2: How do you prioritise your tasks to know which are the most urgent and important?

Doing this will help you establish which tasks you should be working on and what tasks will become the priority in the future.

You will need to regularly review and update each of the boxes. Some of the tasks will disappear as they are completed, and other tasks will need to move into a different box. For example, a task that was 'not urgent and not important' might become urgent and important as the deadline for completion nears.

Larger tasks directly linked to organisational goals will be in the 'important but not urgent' box. These tasks should not be overlooked, even if they are not due to be finished for some time. They may be the tasks that will shape the organisation and if not completed have an impact on its success or failure.

Figure 1: How do you manage the expectations of your colleagues?

Positively manage the expectations of colleagues

Communication is key to managing the expectations of your colleagues, regardless of their level within your organisation. Poor or non-existent communication can cause anxiety and tension among colleagues if they are confused or unsure of what is expected of them. Managers may become frustrated with your lack of communication or concerned that you are not able to manage.

Do not wait until situations become difficult. Keep everyone updated with what is happening and any action that you are currently or will soon be taking. Use the suggestions in Figure 1 to help to manage the expectations of your colleagues.

What improvements can you make to your time-management?

Setting a positive example for others

Leading by example is a good way of setting a positive example. By getting involved in activities and tasks, those around you will see how you expect a job to be completed. From this, they will feel valued and respected, knowing that you would not ask them to do anything that you would not do.

Some of the most effective ways of leading by example are shown in Figure 2.

Figure 2: How many of these traits do you display when working?

Suggesting improvements to working practices and showing an understanding of implications beyond the immediate environment

In your role as a business administrator, you are likely to make suggestions for improvements to working practices for which you have responsibility. It is useful to first share your ideas to obtain the opinions and feedback of others. You could do this with your colleagues, but you may also share your ideas with clients or suppliers. Your suggestions might have implications that will affect both those in your immediate environment, such as your department or team, and beyond.

Clients

When making suggestions for improvements, you should think about how this might affect your clients or customers. You should ask yourself:

- How will this improvement affect our clients?

- Will there be any benefits to our clients?

- What is the reason for the change?

- How will our clients know about the improvements?

- What methods of communication will you use to communicate the improvements?

- Have you tested the improvements on a small group of clients for their feedback?

Suppliers

You are likely to take a different approach with suppliers. However, you do need to keep them informed of any improvements or changes that will affect them. This will help to maintain your working relationship and ensure that their supply to you is not interrupted or changed in terms of delivery time and price. Communicating changes to suppliers should be done as soon as possible.

Other parts of your organisation

Other departments or areas of your organisation may be affected by your suggestions for improvements. It may be appropriate to seek their opinions and feedback before you make improvements so that any negative impact is minimal.

The improvements may be deemed key to the future of your organisation but they may not be well received. This may be true, for example, if the organisation decides to restructure and people's roles are put at risk of **redundancy**. If this is the case, clear and advance communication can help facilitate change. You may need to use change management models, such as those explored in Chapter 6, to help in any transition period.

Periods of change can be very unsettling for all employees but maintaining a positive example can help your colleagues through the change.

How does your organisation keep its suppliers informed about change?

Key term

Redundancy – When a person's job role no longer exists due to restructuring within the organisation.

Behaviours   **B**

Professionalism – Behaves in a professional way. This includes: personal presentation, respect, respecting and encouraging diversity to cater for wider audiences, punctuality and attitude to colleagues, customers and key stakeholders.

Responsibility – Demonstrates taking responsibility for team performance and quality of projects delivered. Takes a clear interest in seeing that projects are successfully completed and customer requests handled appropriately. Takes initiative to develop own and others' skills and behaviours.

Personal qualities – Shows exemplary qualities that are valued including integrity, reliability, self-motivation, being proactive and a positive attitude. Motivates others where responsibility is shared.

Managing resources

What resources you manage will depend on the industry in which your organisation works. It is important that any resources you manage are sourced from a reliable supplier that gives your organisation value for money. Where cost savings can be made, you should ensure that you will still be receiving the same value for money and quality of goods.

Larger organisations may have buying departments for stationery and other resources, whereas in smaller organisations it may be your responsibility to source and order these supplies.

Resources may include people. You may be responsible for drawing up staff rotas or for ensuring that you have enough staff at work for your department to run efficiently.

Facilities can include meeting rooms, classrooms, hotels, conference centres, etc. Your role may be to source and arrange any of these facilities on behalf of colleagues within your organisation.

Table 3 summarises how you should handle purchasing resources.

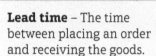

Key term

Lead time – The time between placing an order and receiving the goods.

Identify your requirement, e.g.:	• which stationery items (and quantities) • other organisation-related items • staffing • facilities/room requirements.
Research several suppliers to establish:	• price • value for money • availability • what is included in the price • **lead time** for ordering • terms of business.
Use procurement if appropriate	This is usually for expensive items and/or large quantities. You may have a procurement department who will manage this within your organisation.
Place the order	Your organisation may have a process to place orders which you should use. Keep a record of the orders you place for future reference.

Table 3: Steps involved in purchasing resources

Organising meetings and events

When organising meetings and events, you need to consider several options to ensure that the venue is suitable and will satisfy the needs and purpose of the meeting or event.

Meetings

- **Date and time** – one of the key pieces of information is the date and time. You will need this information before making any further enquires.

- **Venue** – you will need to know where the meeting is to take place. It may be a room within your offices or it may be an off-site location. Your organisation will have a process for booking rooms, which you need to follow. Be sure to book the room and don't take it for granted that a room will be available. Office space can be scarce so you should book as far in advance as possible. If the meeting is to take place off-site, you will need to know the budget available and what would be a suitable location for attendees so that they can get there easily. You may need to consider both public transport for those who do not drive and car parking facilities for drivers.

- **Size of room** – you will need to know the number of attendees so that you know what size meeting room to book. You may also need to consider if any activities will be undertaken during the meeting and if breakout rooms may be required. The layout of the room and the number of tables and/or chairs is also important.

- **Special facilities** – these could include electronic equipment, such as a projector and/or screen.

- **Catering** – catering could include morning coffee, afternoon tea and lunch. You may also need to book refreshments on arrival. Menus will need to be obtained and prices agreed as you will have a budget for the meeting as a whole. You may also need to make provision for any specific dietary requirements.

- **Overnights** – some attendees may need to stay overnight if they have a long journey from home to the venue or if it is a two-day meeting. Again, you will need to establish the budget and suitability of the hotel, making sure it is easy to get to the venue.

Events

- **Venue** – you need to consider the nature of the event, the expected number of attendees, what would be a suitable location and the budget.

- **Exhibitors** – some events may include sponsors or exhibitors. You will need to know the number of exhibitors that the event can accommodate and whether there is a charge for them attending, which might help fund the event. Having exhibitors can take a lot of arranging and you are likely to work within a team if you have to arrange a large event.

- **Catering** – you may not know the exact number of people likely to attend when organising an event and so catering will have to be estimated. For larger events, you may out-source the catering to several mobile outlets offering a variety of dishes. For smaller employee-only events, you may know the numbers and be able to arrange the catering with the venue. They are likely to ask you to confirm a menu in advance.

Behaviours B

Responsibility – Demonstrates taking responsibility for team performance and quality of projects delivered. Takes a clear interest in seeing that projects are successfully completed and customer requests handled appropriately. Takes initiative to develop own and others' skills and behaviours.

Minutes, action logs and logistics

Taking minutes and creating action logs

It is useful to have a written record of what has been discussed during a meeting and who has agreed to undertake the actions. The minutes also serve as a reminder to those who attended the meeting of what was covered and can inform those who were unable to attend the meeting.

During the meeting you are likely to take rough notes that you will 'type up' later and distribute to the relevant people. It is also likely to be your responsibility to file the minutes for future reference.

In order to be effective at taking minutes of meetings, you need to be a good listener and remain focused throughout the meeting. You should be confident in writing things down and be prepared to ask questions when you are unsure or need clarification of the outcome of any discussion topics. It will not be possible to write everything down, so you need to ensure that you capture the key points.

You must be organised from the very beginning of the meeting. A good starting point is to have the agenda to hand and a copy of the minutes from the last meeting so that you can refer to them. You should have enough paper and pens or ensure your laptop or tablet is charged.

There is standard information that you should note for every meeting which includes:

- the name of the group and the date, time and place of the meeting
- the names of attendees, including any guests
- apologies, which is a list of those who were invited but unable to attend.

Organising your notes as you make them will help when you come to finalise them or type them up.

- It is a good idea to give each item a heading. You may also wish to number them.
- Leave a clear space between each of the items in case you need to go back to write in more notes. Underline any important and/or key points.
- Create a system so that you can clearly see any action points agreed and who will be the person to action them.
- If using a loose-leaf pad, ensure that you number each page.

It is important to remember that the minutes are read by people who did not attend the meeting, so when they are finalised you should read through to ensure that they make sense. Meeting attendees may also rely on the minutes to remember the detail of the meeting, particularly any action points and agreed deadlines.

What skills do you use when taking minutes of meetings?

Taking responsibility for logistics

In your role as a business administrator you may be required to take responsibility for **logistics**. You may have to arrange for items to be delivered to customers, or to order and receive items from suppliers. This is arranging the flow of goods from one location to another and could involve a logistics company.

Alternatively, you may be asked to take responsibility for arranging the logistics of a colleague's business-related travel.

Travel

You may be required to make the travel arrangements for colleagues and/or staff in other departments. This could involve arranging any journey, such as booking an air ticket and hiring a vehicle for collection at the destination airport.

If you are responsible for making travel arrangements, you will be required to find the best value for money for the time and date of the travel. You should follow your organisation's travel policies, for example by only booking off-peak rail travel to reduce the cost. You will need to balance this against the required time of arrival for those travelling.

There may be travel forms for individuals to complete which you will use to gather their full travel details.

Accommodation

If you are arranging accommodation, you will need to obtain information about the people travelling such as their name, the duration of their stay, any dietary requirements, the type of room they need and so on. It may be company policy that payment is made by the individual on arrival, or you may need to arrange payment in advance and print off a voucher for the individual to take with them.

Key term

Logistics – Planning carried out in order to move something (usually a product but it may be a person) from one place to another.

Summary

In this section you have learned about how you can take responsibility for planning and organising the many different aspects of your role as a business administrator. You have learned the importance of why you should be organised and how this can help in the day-to-day as well as the more challenging tasks that you will face. This section has covered:

- techniques you can use for taking responsibility for initiating and completing tasks
- how to manage and prioritise your work
- how to manage the expectations of your colleagues of all levels
- key points to consider when leading by example
- suggesting improvements and the implications of them beyond the immediate environment
- ways to manage resources
- organising and arranging meetings, events and logistics
- taking minutes of meetings.

Activities

▶ Activity 1: Initiating and completing tasks

Consider the most recent tasks you have initiated and completed.

Write down the tasks that showcase your ability to plan and achieve the agreed deadlines. Create a table with the following headings:

- Description of the task
- How did you plan it?
- How did you maximise resources while completing the task?
- How were the results of the task achieved?

▶ Activity 2: Managing priorities

Consider the tasks that you have yet to complete. Write a list of these tasks and put them in order of priority.

Speak to your line manager and confirm that you have put your tasks in the correct order of priority. Ask any questions if you are unsure which tasks are the most important.

Check the due dates with others, where appropriate, and check these against your priority list.

Work backwards from the due dates/achievement dates to double check that the tasks are in the correct priority order.

Identify evidence that demonstrates how you have completed the steps in this activity. Include any emails where you have advised people when you will be completing a task.

▶ Activity 3: Positively managing expectations and setting a positive example for others

Practise using the different ways in which you can manage the expectations of others. Write down your findings as you practise. Answer the following questions:

- Whose expectations did you manage?
- What is their role?
- Which technique did you use?
- What did you do to use this technique?
- What was the outcome?

Practise using these ways in which you can lead by example:

- Joining in the operations
- Being aware of what you say
- Listening to others
- Taking responsibility
- Respecting the chain of command
- Avoiding micro-managing
- Being aware of your impact
- Being aware of your actions

Record how you used each way of leading by example and what the outcome was.

▶ Activity 4: Making suggestions for improvements

Think about your current working practices and where you feel improvements could be made. This could be improvements that affect clients, suppliers or other areas within your own organisation. Choose one of your ideas and complete the following.

1. Write down your suggestion and the reason for the improvement.

2. Speak to others to find out their opinions and obtain their feedback on your suggestions.

3. Make a list of people who the improvement is likely to affect.

4. Decide on the message you will send to those on your list.

5. Put a plan together on how you will communicate the improvement and your message.

▶ Activity 5: Managing resources and taking responsibility for logistics

Obtain a copy of your organisational processes and procedures for:

- managing resources
- organising meetings and events
- taking responsibility for logistics, e.g. booking travel and accommodation.

Choose one of the above and gather evidence of how you have followed the process/procedure. The evidence may include emails, booking forms, request forms from colleagues, suppliers' notices, booking confirmations and so on.

▶ Activity 6: Taking minutes during meetings

Think about recent meetings where you have taken the minutes and created an action log. Record:

- the details of the meeting
- how you got organised in advance of the meeting
- essential information you included in the minutes, e.g. list of attendees, etc.
- how you took rough notes
- questions you asked during the meeting
- any points you needed to clarify
- skills you demonstrated during the meeting
- actions you took after the meeting.

Topic consolidation

▶ Test yourself

1. When initiating a task that you will be responsible for, it helps if you:
   - ☐ always make yourself available.
   - ☐ find out who is at fault if mistakes are made.
   - ☐ stay interested in your work.
   - ☐ hold lots of meetings.

2. To manage priorities, it is important that you:
   - ☐ distinguish between urgent and important tasks.
   - ☐ get everything done on your 'to do list', then the important jobs will get done.
   - ☐ give yourself time off.
   - ☐ find plausible excuses when you get behind.

3. When managing the expectation of colleagues, it helps if you:
   - ☐ shield colleagues from unrealistic deadlines.
   - ☐ keep your manager at a distance.
   - ☐ calibrate workloads.
   - ☐ keep a sense of humour.

4. When leading by example, it is useful to:
   - ☐ micro-manage.
   - ☐ stay away from the operations.
   - ☐ never take responsibility.
   - ☐ be aware of what you say.

5. When making suggestions for improvement, you can reduce negative impacts by:
   - ☐ just making an announcement as everyone will soon get used to them.
   - ☐ asking for opinions and feedback about the suggested improvements.
   - ☐ taking time off when the improvement goes live.
   - ☐ delegating communications.

6. When organising meetings, you need to consider:
   - ☐ the number of attendees.
   - ☐ vehicle hire.
   - ☐ who might be on holiday.
   - ☐ the agenda.

7. When taking minutes during meetings and creating action logs you should:
   - ☐ give each section within your notes a heading.
   - ☐ write neatly so that you can use your notes for distribution.
   - ☐ only include those who attended on the minutes.
   - ☐ not include deadline dates on action logs – the individuals will complete this.

8. When planning travel, you should:
   - ☐ always find the cheapest option.
   - ☐ only arrange travel outside peak times.
   - ☐ only arrange travel in peak times.
   - ☐ balance the need of the individual against the best value for money.

16

Project management

Project management

At work, you need to be able to use relevant project management principles and tools to help you scope, plan, monitor and report. You should be able to demonstrate your knowledge and present information about:

- planning and managing projects, including describing what made them successful
- leading small projects and demonstrating leadership skills when managing a project
- your understanding of project management tools and principles.

Planning and managing projects

Being able to plan and manage a project, regardless of its size, is an important skill that you need to develop and demonstrate as part of your apprenticeship.

The project life cycle

The project life cycle helps organisations plan for change and allows managers or administrators to efficiently maintain control of a project.

Every project's life cycle will be different but by using the life cycle to plan each of the stages it will help to test scenarios and keep the project on schedule and to the standard required.

Initiation

This is the first stage where the remit of the project is agreed and includes identifying:

- **aims** and **objectives**
- the scope or purpose of the project
- the roles and responsibilities of those involved
- timescales and associated communication.

It is critical to be clear about what the project's goal is. Without this clarity, it is impossible to measure whether the project eventually achieved its goal.

It is important that the project has established timelines with appropriate deadlines to ensure it keeps to time. If deadlines are not set, the timeline for the project may drift. It is also important that alerts are used to flag up if deadlines are missed.

This primary stage is when **feasibility studies** are carried out to establish if the project should go ahead at all. This can often result in requests for **project proposals** justifying the need for the project.

Planning

The planning stage of the project is vital. It covers all the elements of what the project is going to seek to achieve and the resources that are needed to complete it. The types of plan involved in a project are shown in Table 1.

Key terms

Aims – Overarching goals for the project.

Objectives – Detailed plans for the project leading to the achievement of the aims.

Feasibility study – The consideration of whether a project should go ahead. It identifies everything that is required to make a project work.

Project proposal – The formal process of putting the project forward, including the benefits and any drawbacks of undertaking the project in the first place.

Type of plan	Purpose
Project	This plan covers the overall purpose of the project, its aims and objectives, and the steps that are required during the project's life cycle.
Resource	This plan covers all the human, buildings and equipment resources that are needed for the project, including information about leases, skills of individuals, payments, etc.
Finance	This plan covers the expected income and expenditure, including cash flow forecasting which will ensure that the project can pay its bills along the way. The finance plan also includes a **return on investment** for the project as this will show that it is worth doing. This may not necessarily mean that the project is expected to make a profit as the return on investment may be related to doing good work for a community or another charitable purpose.
Quality	Quality plans include targets for completion, state how **quality assurance** and **quality control** are going to take place, and often include the key elements of success from the perspective of the customer or stakeholder group for whom the project is being undertaken.
Risk	It is important to control risks or review them to put in place **control measures** that try to reduce those that are identified as 'high risk'. Risks can be anything from equipment not arriving on time to bad feedback and publicity being received from stakeholders. Having the risks identified and planned for means their impact is likely to be lower if they happen.

Table 1: Different plans involved in a project

Key terms

Return on investment – An analysis of the expected benefits of carrying out a project against the cost of running the project.

Quality assurance – Checking quality on an ongoing basis against targets or judging fitness for purpose using regular inspections.

Quality control – Measures used to check the quality, such as that raw materials are up to standard.

Control measures – Steps taken to remove or reduce risks that would negatively affect the project.

Execution

This is when the plan is in progress. There should be regular reports to the project team on how things are going. These may be online updates via software or they may be presented through meetings or by attending project briefings.

Monitoring and controlling the project's progress is critical at this stage and careful review of the risk plan and managing the risks is important. You learned about contingency planning and control measures in Chapter 6. It is during the project's execution stage that these are vital and communicating any changes is crucial.

Effective time management is also critical. Any small delay can negatively impact a project and therefore cost the organisation time and money.

Closure and evaluation

Once the project is completed, it is important to review what happened. Here you can measure the outcomes against the original project plan and the aims and objectives that were specified at the beginning of the project.

This is also the stage when any recommendations or different ways of doing things can be noted so that they can be applied to future projects. These are often called 'lessons learned'.

Leading projects and demonstrating leadership skills

Behaviours

Responsibility – Demonstrates taking responsibility for team performance and quality of projects delivered. Takes a clear interest in seeing that projects are successfully completed and customer requests handled appropriately. Takes initiative to develop own and others' skills and behaviours.

Leadership skills are very important as they can make the difference between a successful project and a failure. Being able to plan and manage through good leadership is an essential business administration skill that you need.

Leading projects

Leading projects means you can show that a project you are responsible for is going to be completed in a structured and efficient way. This should involve your team feeling that they are strongly led.

Strong leadership skills for project management are commonly considered in seven categories (shown in Table 2), although there are others that may be important in your organisation and in your sector. You will need to be familiar with each and understand what each means, as well as thinking of others that are unique to your organisation.

Consider your own experience of leading projects. How can you improve?

Leadership skill	How this influences the way you work as the project leader
Listening	You need to show that you can listen carefully and respond to what is being said. Many people listen then respond, but strong leaders listen and then consider the response later.
Negotiating	You need to show that you can make changes to budget, timing and/or the way a task is carried out through negotiation and to the benefit of who you are working with and/or for.
Influencing	You need to show that you can positively influence others to provide their support for your project, to help shape it to have the best possible result or to get additional resources or time.
Motivating	You need to show that you are strong when working with your team, regardless of its size. Motivating others means they will work harder for you and want to get the job done. Strong leaders rely on this.
Inspiring	Having a project is one aspect of leadership but ensuring that others want to get involved, develop their ideas and can think into the future is key and a strong leadership skill.
Innovating	Choosing to do something in a different way requires change, so a strong leader can look at all possibilities and move forward with strength and new ideas.
Team building	Leadership of a project is important for the whole team as the skills of a team are greater when combined than the skills of the individuals in that team.

Table 2: Leadership skills needed in project management

How do you work in a team in your organisation?

Demonstrating understanding of project management tools and principles (1)

Project management tools and principles are essential for good project management. They will support you and help ensure you manage projects effectively.

Project management tools and principles

To help manage projects effectively there are many different tools that you can use. There are six project management tools in particular that you need to be aware of and be able to apply in your administrative role: SWOT analysis, the stakeholder matrix, SMART objectives, Gantt chart, RACI matrix and critical path analysis.

SWOT analysis

SWOT analysis is a common business tool that can be applied to a project. It considers the strengths, weaknesses, opportunities and threats of a project.

A project team or project leader can identify areas of risk in a project and then make improvements to reduce them. The opportunities highlight where additional benefits can be made and the threats show where a project may be held back.

A simplified example of SWOT is shown in Figure 1.

Project: Help the Homeless

Aim: to raise £1000 for a local homeless charity through an open day

Strengths	**Weaknesses**
Positive publicity for the organisation.	Competing for attention with other projects within the organisation.
Homeless people supported locally.	Lack of time for planning.
Opportunities	**Threats**
Use of online methods to promote the project.	Other open days being held in alternative locations (competition).
Partnership working with another organisation to strengthen the relationship.	The potential for bad weather on the day of the event.

Figure 1: A SWOT analysis

Stakeholder matrix

Stakeholder matrices can take slightly different forms but a common and useful version is measuring the power and interest of stakeholders in a project (see Figure 2 for an example). What you show in each direction in the matrix can be changed depending on what is important for a project. Each stakeholder is placed in a section based on the type of project that is being reviewed and their interest in it.

Power and influence		
↑	High power/influence and low interest (satisfy their needs) e.g. local council	High power and high interest (key stakeholder to support) e.g. owners or shareholders
	Low power and low interest (least important) e.g. local community	Low power and high interest (keep them informed and consider) e.g. employees
	Interest →	

Figure 2: A stakeholder matrix

SMART objectives

Setting detailed targets that can be reviewed regularly to check progress is commonly done as part of the project plan. Objectives provide the detailed support that can provide the steps to achieving an overall aim and with quality assurance. The best type of objective is a SMART objective.

- **S**pecific – the objective needs to be precise so that the project team is clear about what needs to be done.
- **M**easurable – the objective must include details that can be measured later, for example sales or an amount of money raised.
- **A**chievable – it must be possible to achieve the objective within the time given. Unachievable objectives provide unachievable results and demotivate team members.
- **R**ealistic – this means that the team must have the necessary skills and knowledge to complete the objective using the expected resources.
- **T**ime-bound – timescales must be appropriate so that the objective can be met but not too easy so that the project takes too long or doesn't have enough impact.

Demonstrating understanding of project management tools and principles (2)

Using project management tools can help you be more organised and effective in your administrative role. The benefits and drawbacks of each can determine whether you should apply them regularly or occasionally in your role.

RACI matrix

An RACI matrix is designed to assign different tasks, responsibilities and decision making to members of a project team. It shows who has been delegated which responsibilities so that the project manager can set expectations for everyone for the duration of the project.

- **Responsible** – this shows who is responsible for a task. Usually this is one person to avoid confusion.

- **Accountable** – this is the person who is accountable for making sure that the task is achieved and approves the work. It may not be the person who does the work but who is accountable for it.

- **Consulted** – this provides information to ensure that others involved or affected by the project are aware of events, and their views and ideas can be considered.

- **Informed** – this means that people are being informed and kept aware of what is happening on the project.

Being clear about who is carrying out tasks, the expectations of each person and the tasks themselves means that the project can be more easily managed and monitored.

Each of the tasks are described in the RACI matrix and then a letter indicating the involvement of the project team is added: R = responsible; A = accountable; C = consulted; and I = informed. An example RACI matrix is shown in Figure 3.

Project task	Project leader	Project member A	Project member B	Project member C	Project member D	Project member E
Task 1	A	I	C	R	I	I
Task 2	C	A	R	I	C	C
Task 3	A	C	I	R	I	C
Task 4	A	R	C	C	I	C

Figure 3: An example of an RACI matrix

Key term

Accountable – The person who is required to justify actions or be responsible for decisions that have been made.

Behaviours

Professionalism – Behaves in a professional way. This includes: personal presentation, respect, respecting and encouraging diversity to cater for wider audiences, punctuality and attitude to colleagues, customers and key stakeholders. Adheres to the organisation's code of conduct for professional use of social media. Acts as a role model, contributing to team cohesion and productivity – representing the positive aspects of team culture and respectfully challenging inappropriate prevailing cultures.

When complete the matrix needs to be shared with all the members of the team so they are clear about their involvement with each task. Tasks can be given to project team members but different roles can also be assigned to them. Being clear with each of the members of the team about who has which responsibility and ensuring that everyone knows what is happening means expectations can be managed.

RACI matrices also mean that everyone is clear about the different tasks required for the project as each has to be listed and described before they can be allocated. Listing and describing tasks makes project management easier if they link back to the project's overall aims, objectives and steps. Describing the activities and completing the table also helps the project leader review what needs to be done and have others give feedback.

Gantt charts

A Gantt chart graphically represents the project's timeline; Figure 4 shows an example. They show how long tasks take individually but also brings the steps of the project into one place. These charts can show critical points where if one task is not completed another cannot happen. Project managers can use Gantt charts to monitor different team members and their involvement in the project, and to make contingency plans in case projects fall behind schedule.

Gantt charts also give project leaders a graphical way to view how the project is progressing. They show points where there may be a need for extra resources and help show that the project leader is organised and efficient. However, they can become complex and need updating frequently to ensure they are still accurate.

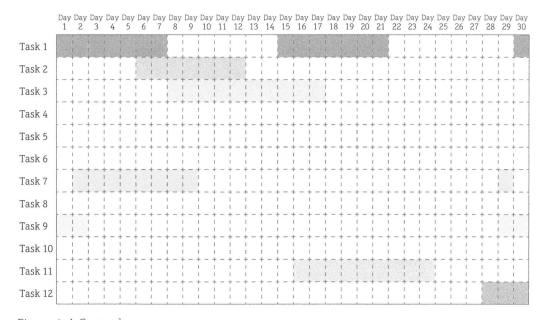

Figure 4: A Gantt chart

Network analysis – Breaking down a project into its parts, including timings, that show where the parts depend on each other to move forward.

Critical path analysis

Critical path analysis (CPA) helps organisations to plan by using a **network analysis** to work out how long it will take to undertake a task and how sensitive an overall project is to time issues.

To carry out a critical path analysis for your project, you need to have a list of all the tasks that you need to complete during the project, the time that each task will take to complete, and knowledge of which tasks affect others so that they depend on each other. In many ways CPA works like a Gantt chart but instead of using bars of time it uses symbols and network diagrams to show the relationships and dependencies of the different activities. An example is shown in Figure 5.

CPA works out the longest path (or the longest period of time) for undertaking all the tasks and the shortest possible date for each task starting and finishing without the project being delayed. Each task needs to be carefully assessed; the quality of that assessment will influence how good the CPA is but the project will still need to be well managed.

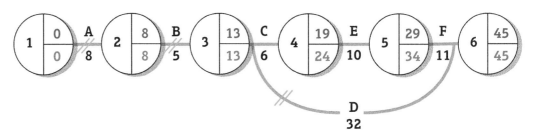

Figure 5: Critical path analysis

Summary

In this section you have learned how project management helps to organise projects and review what is involved. It has covered:

- project management principles and tools used to help scope, plan, monitor and report
- planning resources required to successfully deliver projects
- skills needed to successfully lead projects.

Activities

▶ Activity 1: Researching and reviewing project planning at work

Having deadline alerts for projects can really help to avoid projects getting behind their schedule.

Carry out research into different methods and software packages that can be used to help with this process. Write up your findings into a report.

Add information about your own organisation into your report, including the tools that you usually use at work and the strengths and weaknesses of each.

Share your report with your line manager and add a copy to your portfolio.

▶ Activity 2: Reviewing your leadership skills

Using the information in this chapter about the seven leadership skills demonstrated by strong leaders, produce a self-assessment grid rating yourself against each of those skills. Identify where you have strong skills and where you need to develop. Print a copy of your self-assessment grid.

Now write an action plan for how you could improve the skills that you think are your areas for development.

Share your assessment grid and your action plan with your line manager and ask them to comment. Write a written statement on the meeting and add all three documents to your portfolio. If possible, ask your line manager to write a statement about your grid and action plan, again to add to your portfolio.

▶ Activity 3: Applying project management tools and principles

Choose three project management tools that you either use at work or have learned about in this chapter, i.e. SWOT analysis, a stakeholder matrix, critical path analysis, SMART objectives or a RACI matrix.

Think of a project that you are planning and then apply these tools to that project. Consider which are most appropriate for your organisation.

For each tool, once applied to your project, consider the benefits and drawbacks annotating your final applied tool on a printout.

Produce a written statement comparing the models and their relative use compared with each other. Add the statement to your portfolio.

Discuss your annotated copies with your line manager and then ask them for a statement to go into your portfolio about your understanding of each.

▶ Activity 4: Comparing project management tools

Consider the strengths and weaknesses of two project management tools by comparing them.

Write a list for two of what has worked best for each and a list for what has not worked so well.

Give examples of when each tool has been used to the best effect.

Discuss your comparison with your line manager. Add a copy of your comparison and make notes of your discussion to be added to your portfolio.

Topic consolidation

▶ Test yourself

1. The last stage of project planning is:
   - ☐ initiation.
   - ☐ execution.
   - ☐ planning.
   - ☐ evaluation.

2. Quality control means:
   - ☐ checking quality at the start of a process.
   - ☐ checking quality at the end of the process.
   - ☐ checking quality during the process.
   - ☐ checking quality before the process starts.

3. One benefit of having a risk plan is that:
   - ☐ risks are not considered for a project.
   - ☐ the lowest risks are reviewed.
   - ☐ costs can be controlled.
   - ☐ risks are identified and planned for.

4. Motivating is a key skill for project management because:
   - ☐ it makes team leaders popular.
   - ☐ it avoids employees not understanding.
   - ☐ other team members will work harder for their leader.
   - ☐ it causes conflict amongst employees.

5. SMART means:
   - ☐ specific, meaningful, achievable, realistic, timely.
   - ☐ specific, measurable, accessible, realistic, timely.
   - ☐ specific, measurable, achievable, realistic, timely.
   - ☐ specific, measurable, achievable, random, timely.

6. The benefit for an organisation of using a RACI matrix is:
   - ☐ employees are clear about the planning cycle.
   - ☐ employees are clear about deadlines that affect their work.
   - ☐ employees are clear about their line management.
   - ☐ employees are clear about who has responsibility.

Glossary

Absenteeism – Employees staying away from work without good reason. This is often more common during periods of change.

Accountable – Required to justify actions or be responsible for decisions that have been made.

Accounting transaction – The event and record of goods or services for money. It may be a purchase (buying) or a sale (selling).

Aims – The detailed plans for your organisation's future or project. What does it hope to achieve over the next five years and why?

Anomalies – Things that are not standard, normal or expected.

Appraisal – A review of the employee's work designed to give feedback and identify areas for improvement.

Assets – Resources that hold value to the organisation.
- **Current assets** – can be converted to cash quickly (e.g. products in stock for sale).
- **Fixed assets** – are land, equipment or buildings that can be valued but would take longer to be turned into cash.

Autonomously – Freedom to act independently.

Beliefs – Can be associated with religions or an opinion that is considered to be true.

Bespoke – Systems or software that have been designed specifically for an organisation, commonly designed and maintained by IT staff .

Body language – The use of movement or the body to communicate attitudes and feelings.

Brainstorming – Developing and analysing creative ideas.

Break-even – When an organisation's costs equal its income, it is making neither a profit nor a loss.

Budget holder – The person in charge of a particular budget.

Budgets – Plans that show forecast money coming into the organisation (e.g. sales or grants) or money going out (e.g. costs).

Business case or **project proposal** – The formal process of putting the concept forward, including stating the benefits and any drawbacks of undertaking the project in the first place.

Cash – The amount of physical money in the bank.

Cash flow – The amount of cash moving in and out of the organisation during a given period of time.

Class – The group that individuals fall into based on their education and/or wealth. People are often said to be working class, middle class or upper class.

Cloud-based – Software that runs over the internet.

Coaching – Facilitating and developing skills in others.

Collaboration – Working with someone or a team of other people to produce something.

Competitive – The organisation being as good as (or better than) its rivals and competitors so that customers or clients choose your organisation.

Confidence – Faith in your own skills, qualities and ability.

Conflict – A serious disagreement between two parties.

Consent – Means that people agree to their data being held, being clear about opting in and giving them choice and control over their personal data.

Consumer price index (CPI) – A measure that looks at the price of all items that we spend money on, including food, clothing and entertainment, but which does not include the amount we spend on housing and mortgages.

Contingency planning – Making plans to cope with an event or risk that could happen but is not expected.

Continuous review – Constantly noting or checking progress, rather than doing it just once at a set time.

Contract – Means that employers need to process personal data in order to fulfil their contractual obligations.

Control measures – Steps taken to remove or reduce risks that would negatively affect the project.

Credit note – A statement given to the organisation or customer when goods have been returned. The value can be used for future purchases.

Glossary

Cyber security – The protection of IT systems from theft or damage caused to hardware, software and electronic data.

Data controller – Someone who determines the purpose and way of processing data.

Data processors – The people that work on behalf of a controller and actually process the data.

Defer – To put off or postpone an action or event until a later time.

Demand – The number of people or organisations wanting goods or services.

Demographics – The breakdown of a country's population into different characteristic groups, such as by gender, age or income.

DSE – Display screen equipment.

Dividends – A share of the profits that are paid to shareholders each year.

Economic environment – The economy considered as a whole.

Economic growth – An increase in the value of goods and services produced by the country.

Economies of scale – Being able to pay a cheaper price for something because it is bought in bulk.

Emotional intelligence – Being aware of and being able to control your own emotions.

Empathy – The ability to understand and share other people's feelings.

Employee empowerment – When employees are given the power to have greater influence over their role, e.g. by making decisions (within guidelines).

Employee engagement – When an organisation gets its employees interested and involved in their roles at work.

Employment tribunal – Can be used if an employee has been unable to solve their equality issues in the workplace. This makes their complaint more formal and compensation may be awarded.

Environmental sustainability – Making sure that organisations use resources that are renewable or recyclable.

Ethical standards – Principles related to the way that organisations operate that generate higher levels of trust, openness and honesty by taking good decisions in the best interests of the organisation and others in society.

External audit – Engaging accountants from outside the organisation to check that the accounts produced are true and fair.

Feasibility study – The consideration of whether a project should go ahead. It identifies everything that is required to make a project work.

Fiscal policy – The amount of money that the government spends or receives in taxes that it uses to help grow or shrink the economy.

Formal communication – Communication through the organisation's official channels.

Formality – In business, means how traditional or conventional the conduct situation must be.

4G – Broadband networks which are present in the UK to link mobile devices. The 'next generation' will be 5G.

GDPR – The General Data Protection Regulation.

General election – Happens at least every five years when everyone who is of voting age and registered to vote can choose the candidate that they want to represent their local area in the House of Commons.

Government spending – Any money that is paid out to the public sector directly to run services, or to the private sector to invest in the UK as a whole.

Gross domestic product (GDP) – The value of all the goods and services produced within a certain time period (often a quarter or year) by individuals and organisations. It is possible to compare the GDP for different countries.

Harassment – Violating your dignity or creating an offensive environment for you based on your protected characteristic.

Harm – The damage done to someone or something that has suffered injury, maltreatment or loss.

Hazard – Anything that may cause harm.

Household income – Measures the amount of money in a household that is available to spend, after considering tax and benefits; this money is called **disposable income**.

Identifier – A piece of data that identifies one individual from another, for example their name or their Internet Protocol (IP) address.

Induction – Training given for new employees joining a job role to enable them to do their work.

Inflation – The general rise in average prices in a country.

Informal communication – Communication through unofficial channels such as rumours, gossip and chats at the coffee machine.

Internal audit – Checking controls that an organisation has in place for recording that transactions are working.

International relations – The term used for the relationship between two or more countries from a political, economic and cultural perspective.

Interpersonal skills – The skills used to interact and communicate with others.

Intervention – In politics, the degree to which government tries to 'control' the economy.

Inventory – The amount of a product that an organisation has in stock.

Jargon – Words or expressions used by a profession or group that are difficult for others to understand.

Joint procurement – Two organisations, working in partnership, to purchase goods or services at a lower price than they would get if buying alone.

Labour market – The number of people who are available for work in an economy and the number of organisations that are wanting people to work for them.

Lead time – The time between placing an order and receiving the goods.

Liabilities – Money that the organisation owes.

• **Short-term/current liabilities** – usually need to be paid within one year.

• **Long-term liabilities** – for example a mortgage or loan, paid over many years.

Logistics – Planning carried out in order to move something (usually a product but may be a person) from one place to another.

Manual Handling Operations Regulations 1992 – Require organisations to avoid moving objects if they can but also to train you how to move them appropriately and without causing harm to yourself or others.

Market forces – The way that buyers and sellers behave in a type of market.

Mitigation – Acting to reduce the chances of something bad happening.

Monetary policy – The process that the Bank of England uses to control the UK economy, such as setting the base rate from which all other interest rates are set.

More favourable treatment – When one person is treated better than another.

Motivation – Making employees feel more strongly that they want to achieve something because they are happy or driven to succeed.

Near miss reporting – Informing a relevant department that you have nearly had an accident or injury.

Network analysis – Breaking down a project into its parts, including timings, to show which of the parts depend on each other to move forward.

Objectives – Detailed plans for the project that lead to the achievement of the aims.

Office for National Statistics (ONS) – The body that produces official statistics for the UK.

Operational improvements – Improvements to any aspect of the day-to-day running or operations of the organisation.

Opportunity cost – The loss of other, more profitable alternatives when you have to do something else instead.

Organisational restructure – When an organisation changes the number of employees that it requires within its structure or moves them to different areas of the organisation.

Passive – Accepting something without reacting.

Perception – Means that someone thinks you are (or are not), have (or have not) that protected characteristic, and as a result discriminates against you.

Personal data breach – A lapse in security leading to accidental or deliberate destruction, loss, change, unauthorised change or access to personal data.

PESTLE analysis – An analytical tool used to consider all the external factors that affect an organisation, project or idea.

Political environment – Government actions that affect the operations of a company or business.

Positive action – When an employer takes steps to encourage people from disadvantaged backgrounds to take up opportunities where they are suitably qualified.

Prime minister – The leader of the political party that wins the most seats in a general election.

Privacy notice – A statement about how data protection principles will be applied when processing the data. They should be clear and to the point.

Private sector – Organisations that are owned by private individuals or shareholders. It covers small to very large organisations. These organisations are not government owned or controlled.

Procurement – Selecting suppliers and obtaining goods.

Project proposal – The formal process of putting the project forward, including the benefits and any drawbacks of undertaking the project in the first place.

Protected characteristic – One of the characteristics protected by the Equality Act – a person with that characteristic is protected from discrimination.

Public sector – Relates to organisations that are run by or for the government (either national or local) and are funded through taxes and national contributions.

Public services or **public sector** – Services that are organised by the government to help the community, such as healthcare, colleges, the police and road maintenance.

Purpose and activities – The purpose of an organisation answers the question: what does my organisation do? Why does your organisation exist? Is it to make a profit, provide a service, help a certain sector of society, etc.? The activities are what it does on a day-to-day basis to achieve its purpose.

Qualitative information – Information based on opinions, thoughts and feelings.

Quality assurance – Checking quality on an ongoing basis against targets or judging fitness for purpose using regular inspections.

Quality control – Measures used to check the quality, for example that raw materials are up to standard.

Quantitative easing – When the Bank of England starts to buy assets from other organisations such as banks to help grow the economy by increasing demand.

Quantitative information – Information based on facts, figures and 'right or wrong' answers.

Rapport – A close relationship where people understand each other's feelings or ideas and communicate well.

Redundancy – When a person's job role no longer exists due to restructuring within the organisation.

Remuneration package – The combined benefits paid to an employee in addition to their salary, such as free gym membership.

Resistance to change – When employees avoid a change or take steps to try to avoid a change happening.

Resources – The elements that are needed to run your organisation, from the computer equipment needed to carry out your administration role (and not just the computer on your desk but the entire IT network) through to the skills of the people who work with you.

Retention policy – Gives details about long information will be kept for and outlines standard retention periods for different types of personal data. The policy should also allow records to be deleted earlier if they are not being used and are no longer required.

Return on investment – An analysis of the expected benefits of carrying out a project against the cost of running the project.

RIDDOR – Reporting of Injuries, Diseases and Dangerous Occurrences Regulations 2013.

Risk – The potential to expose someone or something to danger or loss.

Risk – The chance of something happening.

Role model – A person who is looked at by others to set an example.

Sector – A particular part of the economy. The sector may be huge, for example the public sector, or be further broken down, for example the finance and banking sector is part of the larger private sector.

Social responsibility – Working in the best interests of others in your society.

Society – A group of people that are present in a country or an area, or a particular group within a population.

Special categories of personal data – Include sensitive data about an individual and should only be collected if it is necessary.

Stakeholder – Someone who has an interest in the activities of the organisation.

Supply – The number of organisations offering the goods or services in the market.

Supply chain – All the organisations and people directly or indirectly that help make a product or service and deliver it to the customer. It covers everything from components being produced to getting it to the final customer, e.g. the parcel delivery company that ships a parcel from the manufacturer to the customer.

Surplus – The amount of money that is left over after an organisation has taken its expenses away from its income.

Template – A basic document that provides a framework that can be built on when writing a letter or other business communication.

Tender – To offer or present something formally.

Trade tariffs – Additional taxes that must be paid on imports or exports of goods between different countries. These additional taxes are added to the price of goods but are paid to the government.

Trade war – When countries introduce or raise tariffs between each other to increase trade barriers between them, affecting imports and exports.

Transparent – Communication that is open about why decisions have been made and by whom.

Value added tax (VAT) – A tax added to the cost of some goods and services.

Values – How your organisation behaves. Your organisation may have a set of values that it publishes or adds to its letters and website. These may be simple words or phrases, such as 'We believe in people', 'Straightforward and open minded' or 'Keep it simple'.

Verbal communication – Sharing information between individuals through speech.

Victimisation – When people who are protected from being discriminated against under the act are treated badly because they have made a complaint.

Vision – The longer-term plan of where your organisation sees itself in five or more years' time and what it seeks to achieve. Many larger organisations will have a vision statement or mission explaining what it is trying to achieve, for example to be the best in its sector, and how it can achieve this.

Whistleblowing – Providing information to an appropriate body. Whistleblowers are protected as employees by law.

Workshop – A meeting to have an intensive discussion and analysis of a project or idea.

Written communication – Sharing information in writing.

Zero based budgeting – When a budget is 'reset' every financial year and all items of spending have to be re-justified.

Index

Index